The biases of management

Organizational Behaviour and Management series
Edited by Robert Goffee

Management in Developing Countries series
Edited by Alfred M. Jaeger and Rabindra N. Kanungo

Managing through Organization: the management process, forms of organization and the work of managers
Colin Hales

Organizational Change and the Management of Expertise
Janet Webb and David Cleary

The biases of management

Barbara Wake Carroll

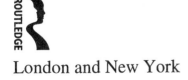

London and New York

First published 1993
by Routledge
11 New Fetter Lane, London EC4P 4EE

Simultaneously published in the USA and Canada
by Routledge
29 West 35th Street, New York, NY 10001

Typeset in Times by LaserScript, Mitcham, Surrey
Printed and bound in Great Britain by
Biddles Ltd, Guildford and King's Lynn

British Library Cataloguing in Publication Data
A catalogue record for this book is available from the British Library.

ISBN 0–415–10196–4

Library of Congress Cataloging in Publication Data
Carroll, Barbara Wake, 1947–
  The biases of management/Barbara Wake Carroll.
  p. cm. – (Organizational behaviour and management series)
  Includes bibliographical references and index.
  ISBN 0–415–10196–4
  1. Management – Philosophy. 2. Prejudice. 3. Decision-making.
  4. Management – Social aspects. I. Title. II. Series.
  HD31.C3497   1993
  658.4 – dc20   93-7408
                                                          CIP

Contents

Figures

Tables

Acknowledgements

Research of this type is obviously not done in isolation. I would like to thank: Professors Russell Stout, Jack Richardson and Terrance G. Carroll for their invaluable advice on the theoretical development of the book; Professor William Frisbee, Professor Tom Muller, Gerald Bierling, Michael Hindmarsh, John Knox, Brenda O'Neill, Richard Powers and the computing staff at the University of Guelph for the many hours helping me with the computer analysis; Helena Mae Wake for meticulously checking the references, any errors which remain are due to my neglect not hers; the librarians at McMaster University, the Canadian Imperial Bank of Commerce, HUD and the Federal Home Loan Bank Board; and finally the many people in the companies – or who knew the companies – who talked to me and listened to my ideas, in particular, my former colleagues at Canada Mortgage and Housing Corporation, and Cecil W., Laurence G., Percival E., Wilfred M. and the late Stanley T. Wake. This research was supported in part by a grant from the Social Sciences and Humanities Research Council of Canada.

1 Introduction
How organizational decisions are made

INTRODUCTION

Managers of large organizations face no shortage of advice on how to run those organizations. There is a huge literature, much of it of a high quality, that prescribes appropriate managerial behaviour in various circumstances. The people who hold senior management positions are usually well educated, experienced and knowledgeable about the internal and external circumstances of their organizations. Frequently they have formal training in the fields of business or public administration. And yet almost everyone who has observed the behaviour of large organizations is aware of instances in which managers have adopted and persisted in a course of action that seems explicable only in terms of some sort of collective suicidal impulse. Lemming-like, such organizations march decisively towards destruction.

One of the continuing problems for managers, and for those who study organizations, is to account for this discrepancy between 'how managers actually react . . . and prescriptions for how they should react' (Whetten 1980: 373). This study focuses on non-rational aspects of management decision-making in an effort to explain this paradox. The basic thesis is that the management group in any organization, as a collective group of individuals, is likely to incorporate within itself deeply rooted biases that reflect the cultural values of the society in which the organization functions, and values produced by the backgrounds of the managers themselves. Furthermore, this type of organizational bias varies from organization to organization in a manner that is at least partly predictable, and that can significantly affect decision-making and organizational performance.

As a matter of convenience, I will often refer to organizations 'taking actions' or 'making decisions'. The emphasis that I place on characteristics of the managers of the organizations should make it clear, however, that this is nothing more than a shorthand way of writing about things which are done by varying groups of individuals within *each* organization. The 'behaviour of an organization' is simply the behaviour of people within it, and – to a large extent – it is the behaviour of the most senior managers that is the key. An organizational bias, then, is a bias shared by its senior managers.

Most management books tell managers how to act. One popular panacea – MBO, 'Excellence', TQM – will take hold and produce a wave of belief, a myth that it can help all firms, all of the time. The problem is that these myths tend to break down in times of crisis because they are either counter-intuitive or force unfamiliar patterns upon the individuals.

This book takes a different approach. It recognizes that people act in specific, non-rational ways as a result of their education, their experience and their values, and suggests means of designing organizations which can accommodate these non-rational biases. It is based upon two studies. One considers objective statistical measures of organizational action over time. The other is broader and looks at a common feature of the management structure found in successful organizations.

By focusing upon characteristics of the senior management group within organizations, I attempt to explain some of the differences among organizations doing similar things and operating in similar environments. The first goal is to show that there is a discernible bias exhibited by organizations which can account for otherwise perverse organizational action, and which can be explained by their management configuration and systemic values. The second goal is to weigh the implications of this finding within the broader context of organizational design and adaptation.

One popular means of responding to unsatisfactory performance levels is to call in management consultants to prescribe solutions. By implication, at least, this study helps to explain why prescriptive attempts to change organizations often fail to lead to improved performance. Models of organizational decision-making rarely consider systematic bias as a source of variations in the outcomes and performance of organizations. Instead, these models and the prescriptive theories that have evolved from them often assume that bias is inevitably short-lived and self-correcting. Alternatively, they may assume a level of altruism or objective rationality on the part of management which, in McGregor's words, is tantamount to asking 'water to flow uphill' (1960: 20).

THE NEO-WEBERIAN MODEL

The neo-Weberian model provides an explanation of how organizations make decisions and how management controls the outcomes of the organization. It is explicitly intended to be a synthesis of the behavioural model of organizations' decision-making and the contingency theories of technological and environmental determinism. While it is largely a rational model

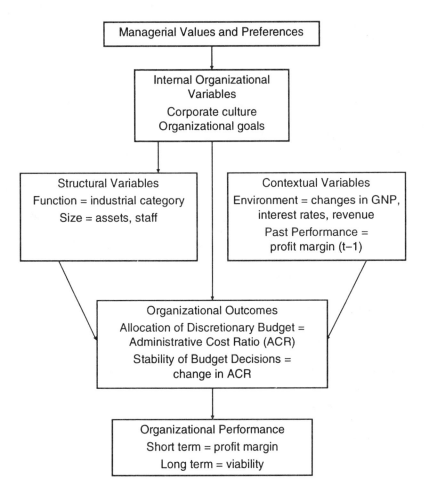

Figure 1.1 The neo-Weberian model

which assumes a logical, explicit connection between information and action, it also recognizes that there are non-rational aspects of decision-making. These include the implicit values of the people who make up the organization, and the constraining effects of structure.

The model, illustrated in Figure 1.1, focuses attention on the role of the management group which determines the day-to-day activities of the organization, and which controls the decision-premises of the organization through control of its structure. It distinguishes between organizational outcomes, which are the decision preferences of managers as they are actually implemented, and organizational performance, which is the attainment of organizational goals, such as profits or the objectives of a policy. It suggests that outcomes and performance are functions of a combination of structural factors, such as size, age and technology; contextual factors, such as the environment and past performance of the organizations; and the goals of the management.

The contingency approach has been declared dead by some authors and criticized on the basis of its empirical validity by others (Carroll 1988b; Fry 1982). It nevertheless remains the most commonly cited perspective, in part because its basic argument contains a simple, compelling logic. Organizations of the same size, operating in the same environment, and doing the same thing, will exhibit similar structures, and be similar in the allocation of their administrative costs (Thompson 1967). Conversely, organizations doing different things (that is, utilizing a different technology), organizations of different sizes, and organizations in different environments, will have different structures. Factors such as size are structural variables which remain relatively constant over time, and can be distinguished from the contextual variables such as past performance and environmental change which are more directly affected by factors external to the organization.[1]

This determination of the organization's structure by these contingency variables is limited, however, by the element of strategic choice left to management (Chandler 1962; Child 1972). Thus, while choice is constrained by environmental and technological factors, there is still some managerial discretion about the precise structural characteristics of the individual organization.

In dealing with managerial choice, however, one aspect which has been largely overlooked is the composition of the management group and, in particular, the relationship between its composition and the sub-systems of the organization. Parsons (1960) and Thompson (1967) both considered the organization to consist of three basic sub-systems – institutional, managerial and technical. These sub-systems act relatively independently, but are linked through boundary-spanning positions and interact in various ways. The institutional sub-system is primarily concerned with the legitimation of the organization, and with cultural values and overall institutional patterns within the wider external environment of the organization. The managerial sub-system is concerned with system maintenance and co-ordination, and with the administration and control of the technical sub-system. The technical sub-system is concerned with the technical production aspects of the organization.

Management, in this context, is not seen as a synonym for the managerial/administrative sub-system of the organization, nor as a single individual, but rather as the grouping of senior executives whose decisions direct the organization. Nor are the various interests of management – institutional, managerial, or technical – assumed to be hierarchical, as is commonly the case in management texts (Daft 1983; Ullrich and Wieland 1980: 27–31). Rather, management is considered to be the most senior executives of the organization, and their interests and backgrounds may be from any combination of these three sub-systems.

It is possible, then, that a tendency to equate management with either a single individual or the managerial sub-system has camouflaged systematic variations in managerial behaviour. Thus, distinguishing between organizations on the basis of the sub-systems represented within their managements could be useful.

By definition, all members of the organization are part of one or more sub-systems. If we use these categories, it is clear that the management can be one of three general types: one restricted to representatives of only a single sub-system; one which is representative of two of the three sub-systems; or one which includes all three. Thus, there are seven types of management configurations which can develop within organizations. These variations are discussed further in Chapter 5.

Empirical tests have supported and refined the neo-Weberian model as a description of how most organizations, and the individuals within them, make decisions about both operational and strategic actions. The decision-making component within the model provides an explanation of how organizations adapt to contextual changes; the structural component provides a predictive element and an explanation for stability. The emphasis upon structural contingency variables and standard operating procedures (or 'rules of thumb') which become institutionalized across groups of firms explains the similarities of firms.

The role of the management provides a dynamic explanation of directed action. The rational manager, faced with an uncertain and unknown environment, adopts and follows standard operating rules. But collectively management will also reform to meet changing circumstances, altering decision rules and search rules to conform to some 'rational norm' represented by the needs of the technology and environment of the organization. If the problems requiring adaptation are spaced to allow time for change, and successive problems requiring adaptation are dealt with smoothly as decision and search rules are modified, the organization will adapt successfully.

But often this does not happen. Organizations continue to use outmoded decision rules; they do not expand their areas of search; and the search for solutions sometimes follows rather than precedes choice (Cyert 1978; Crozier 1964; Downs 1967). Studies which have used the model or some variant of it have tended to concentrate upon short-term decision-making, particularly cases in which the organizations were in crisis or a state of decline. They have also tended to focus upon only one industry, and many have been quasi-public institutions such as hospitals and universities. Few studies have focused upon the management group as an independent variable and attempted to explain or predict their actions across industries and over an extended period of time. This book attempts to do just that.

Before proceeding to test the impact of bias within management, it is appropriate to consider how well the model works as a whole in explaining both the short and long term aspects of decision-making on a broader range of firms.

In attempting to do this, the resource allocation or budgetary decisions, become our focus. Dunbar has defined the budget of the organization as 'the combination of a goal setting and goal achieving machine', a measure of power and control within the organization (1971: 89). It provides a framework of the intended commitments of the organization, and this allocation of dollars and people constitutes a measurable outcome of decisions. As it has been succinctly put: '[t]he manager must put his resources where his mouth is if something is to be considered a goal' (Buck in Mintzberg 1983: 248).

If we are concerned with adaptation, one measure to consider is the size of the administrative component of the organization. The administrative component is the portion of the organization concerned with control and co-ordination rather than production. As it is the most discretionary aspect of an organization's budget, it is also the portion of the organization which should be most amenable to adaptation. The size of the administrative component reflects the preferences of the management, but it is also determined in part by a number of structural factors. For example, while the size of the administrative component of organizations has been found to be related to the technology of the organization, it is also larger in organizations that are older, that are bigger, or that are more complex (Anderson and Warkov 1961; Dunleavy 1989; Meyer 1985; Nystrom and Starbuck 1988; Tainio *et al.* 1991). Each of these factors, then, has some bearing on the proportion of the organization's resources that is allocated to administrative activities. In considering what factors influence an organization's decisions, or the collective decisions of its managers, the portion of the budget allocated to the managerial rather than technical sub-systems becomes an appropriate focus.

The Administrative Cost Ratio (ACR) measures administrative expenditures as a percentage of total expenditures.[2] The willingness of organizations to alter the distribution of their expenditures between the administrative (overhead) and production functions is measured by the change in the ACR from one budgetary year to the next. We want to know, then, the extent to which the model can predict actual budget allocation decisions, and changes in budget allocation decisions.

TESTING THE MODEL

This initial empirical research considers the resource allocation patterns of a sample of thirty-four Canadian and American firms drawn from the real estate development, mortgage financing and banking industries. (Mortgage financing comprises savings and loans companies in the United States and loans and trust companies in Canada.) The data cover the eleven years from 1972 to 1982, a period which encompassed times of both economic growth and decline. The sample included six housing construction and development companies in Canada and five in the US; five banks in each country; and six federally registered loan companies in Canada and seven in the US. (The firms are listed in the Appendix at the end of the book.) These sectors were chosen because they were ones in which the Canadian and American markets were dominated by domestically owned and managed firms and because they were characterized by a high level of technological determinism.[3]

Banking is banking, a mortgage is a mortgage, and a house is a house. These industries differ, however, in the degree to which they are regulated, in their characteristic attitudes towards risk-taking and in their typical internal administrative structures (Meyer 1985: 39). Banking is a highly regulated, risk-adverse industry with firms which are hierarchical and formalized. Housing construction is directly regulated to a considerably lesser degree (Carroll 1988), and is characterized by a much higher level of risk-taking, and a more organic form of organizational structure (Eichler 1982). Loan companies are an intermediate category in each case. The firms within this initial sample also differ in that some have hired, professional managements, while owners play central roles in others.

The basic model summarized in Figure 1.1 suggests that the budgetary decisions or outcomes of the organization will be a function of its size and age, its technology, its past performance, its external environment, and the preferences of its management. The version of the model tested here is simplified by the exclusion of the age of the organization and by the omission of any direct measurement of the goals and roles of their managements.[4] Variations in management will be introduced in later chapters.

In order to test the model, we need measurements for the variables which are objective, internal to the organization, and apparent to the management. Some variables, such as size and performance, have obvious meanings. In this study, size is measured by the assets (in dollars) of the organization. Past performance is indicated by the after-tax return as a percentage of revenue (that is, the profit margin) in the previous year, a commonly used measure of performance. But two variables, 'technology' and 'changes in the external environment' are less self-evident. Technology is defined here simply as the organization's function – residential development, banking,

Table 1.1 Variables by function 1971–82 (mean levels)

	Total	Banks	Loan companies	Development companies
Administrative Cost Ratio (ACR)* (%)	17	23	17	11
Annual change in ACR (%)	0.8	1.8	0.8	0.7
Size (assets in millions)[a]*	11,319	28,980	7,358	700
Environment (% annual change in revenue)	24	28	21	25
Performance (% annual return on revenue)	5	6	6	3
Number	34	10	12	12

Notes: * Differences significant at the 0.05 level (based upon ANOVA).
[a] The size of the organizations is indicated by assets measured in the currency of the country in which they are located.

or mortgages and loans. But how does a manager know or perceive that the external environment is changing? Four possibilities were considered – economic growth rates, inflation rates, interest rates and rates of change in revenues. In interviews, managers said that the most commonly stated measure which would prompt them to reassess their budgetary allocations was changes in revenue. Environmental change, then, is measured by the percentage change in the organization's revenues from the previous year.[5]

Table 1.1 provides the mean levels of the variables for the eleven-year period, both for the sample as a whole, and separately for the firms in each of the three functional sectors. It indicates, for example, that the level of administrative costs (ACR) varies widely across the sectors. The mean level for real estate developers was 11 (that is, 11 per cent of all expenditures were for administration and overhead costs), for loan companies it was 17 and for banks, 23. These levels also vary widely within each sector. U.S. Home, a real estate developer, had a mean ACR level of 22, for example, while Daon Development, a Canadian company of a similar size, had a level of only 2. The variation is not only between firms in different countries. Montreal Trust (assets $8.95 billion) had a mean ACR level of 34, while Canada Trustco (assets $9.41 billion) had a level of only 20. While there is considerable variation among firms in size, the differences in performance, changes in the ACR, and changes in revenue, are not significant among the three functional sectors.

We accept that organizations may occasionally act in random, idio-syncratic or irrational ways in the short term; in the longer term, however, 'norms of rationality' should apply, and organizational decisions should respond to the structural and contextual variables. The length of time that is implied by the 'short term' or 'long term' is not entirely clear. In interviews managers indicated that although there were constraints it was the year-to-year budget which was the focus of their short-term attention: 'when revenues start to slide, you look around to see what you can change.' One year, then, was viewed as the short term and the full eleven-year period as the long term. It does seem reasonable to suppose that, for most organ-izations most of the time, a period of one year should provide sufficient opportunity to recognize and alter decisions that seem inappropriate.

Figure 1.2 provides the results of our long-term test of the model using multiple regression analysis. The numbers on the left of the name of the variable give its relative importance (the standardized regression coefficient) in explaining the level of ACR.[6] The logic of understanding these numbers is quite simple. The larger the number the more important that factor is. Those on the right provide the same information for the change in the level of the ACR. The numbers at the bottom tell us the percentage of the variation among the

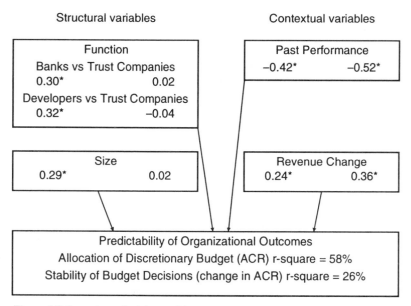

Figure 1.2 Long-term decision-making

Note: *Statistically significant at 0.05 level.

firms which is explained. In other words, we are asking if the model can explain differences in the average budgetary allocations of these firms over the course of more than a decade, a period that is certainly long enough to permit 'norms of rationality' to apply.

The most important finding is that the model does explain a considerable amount, confirming that in the long run firms do conform to some 'norm of rationality'. Over time, the model can predict 58 per cent of the variation in the ACR level, but only 26 per cent of the variation in changes in the ACR level. For the level of the ACR, all of the variables contribute to this explanation with the contextual variables somewhat stronger and the structural variables relatively equal. For the change in ACR, as you would expect, only the contextual variables are relevant. Past performance is almost twice as powerful a predictor as revenue change, and its effect is negative, indicating that a decline in profits one year will prompt an increase in administrative costs in the following year, and vice versa.

On the other hand, as revenues rise so do administrative cost levels and vice versa. While the latter observation is consistent with a rational model, the effects of past performance are less so at first glance. Certainly if more money is available one would expect more money to be devoted to

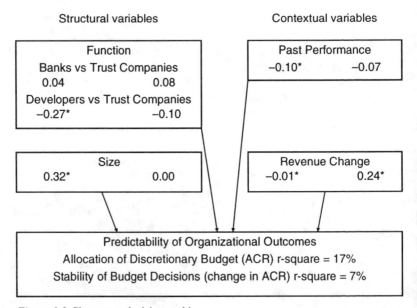

Figure 1.3 Short-term decision-making

Note: *Statistically significant at 0.05 level.

overhead costs or 'slack'. But why would this also be true when profits decline? A rational answer may be that a decrease in profits prompts managers to devote more money to co-ordination and control costs in an effort to improve efficiency.

Figure 1.3 provides the results for the shorter-term, year-to-year variations in the budgetary allocations of organizations using the annual values for each variable and each firm. They confirm what others have found: the model is weak in predicting short-term adaptation. For annual ACR levels, the effectiveness of the model falls to 17 per cent. More importantly, the level of the ACR seems to be influenced entirely by the two structural variables – size and function – giving support to the argument that organizations do not adapt to short term change in a rational fashion. We can now explain only 6 per cent of the change in ACR, with revenue change the only factor which has influence.

On the whole, then, the model is reasonably successful in accounting for variations in the mean level of firms' administrative costs over the long term and has a certain intuitive logic. Companies that operate in particular functional sectors (banking or lending), that are bigger, and that have poorer past performance records, tend to allocate greater proportions of their budgets to administrative costs. In the short term, the firm does not alter its overall level of administrative costs to reflect changes in either revenue or performance.

When separate analyses are carried out for each of the three industrial sectors, the power of the model varies considerably with function. In the case of banks and development companies the power and impact of the variables are similar to the findings for sample as a whole, although the model is more powerful for banks than for the development companies. In the case of the loan companies, however, the model has virtually no ability at all to account for variations in the ACR levels, or changes in the ACR. For the banks, this might indicate that large formalized firms act in a more 'rational' fashion, or have some other similarity that affects their decision-making patterns such that they conform more closely to the expectations of the model. For developers it may be that they operate with so little slack in their operations that they must be very careful to act 'rationally'. It may also say something about the management of loans companies who seem to act in such unpredictable ways. We will return to this point later.

The figures also do not fully display the complex relationship between the structural variables and the ACR. As we saw in Table 1.1, banks tend to devote the highest proportions of their budgets to administrative costs, followed by loan companies, while developers tend to have significantly lower ACR levels. The effects of size are contingent upon function. Among loan companies and developers, the bigger firms tend to have *higher* ACR

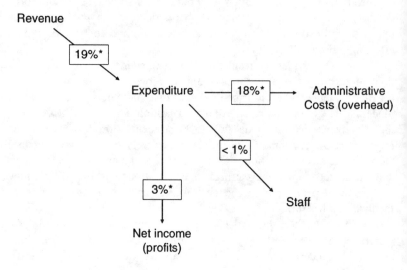

Figure 1.4 Path of decision-making

Notes: Statistics are r-square values showing the percentage of the variation in the rates of
change of pairs of variables which can be statistically explained.
*Significant at 0.05 level.

levels than smaller firms in the same industries, but bigger banks tend to
have *lower* ACR levels than smaller banks. This is also not unexpected. A
very small developer with a very small staff would have little administrative overhead. In their earliest days in the industry some of these firms
were literally a family business with the owners doing everything but keep
the books – which were done by their wives. On the other end of the
extreme the very largest banks experience economies of scale which allow
them to lower their administrative costs.

Finally, there is the question of what aspects of an organization are most
likely to be altered when budget decisions are made. When revenues change
and a manager reassesses budgetary allocations, what does he or she alter? It
would be reasonable to expect that expenditures would change with revenue.
But would staff numbers also change? or other overall administrative costs?
or after tax income? Figure 1.4 provides a diagram of the order of this
decision path and the per cent of correlation between each of the factors.

The most important aspect to note is simply the very low level of the
correlations. Environmental change, which is measured by change in
revenues, can account for 19 per cent of the variation in rates of change in
expenditures, and changing expenditures in turn can account for 18 per cent

of the variation in firms' changes in administrative costs. Turning this around, over 80 per cent of the variation in spending on administration is *unrelated* to any corresponding change in total expenditure levels. Similarly, more than 80 per cent of the variation in total expenditures *cannot* be explained by any corresponding change in revenues.

Changes in a firm's size or revenues have only limited implications for total spending, and almost no impact on changes in staffing and budgetary allocations. These internal changes in expenditures, staffing and budgetary allocations in turn have little relationship to after-tax income. With the modest, partial exceptions that have been noted, each of these variables tends to change in ways that are quite independent of changes in the other factors. In part, this undoubtedly reflects the fact that expenditure levels, staff numbers, and administrative costs all include major items which are inelastic or non-discretionary, at least in the short term. Nevertheless, the overall weakness of the relationships reinforces the notion that we need to look to factors other than those included in the analysis thus far, if we hope to develop a more complete explanation for differences in the decisions that organizations make.

This preliminary empirical test considers only one form of budgetary decision-making among a small but diverse group of firms, but it shows that the neo-Weberian model is a moderately good predictor of the budgetary decision outcomes of organizations under long-term 'norms of rationality'. It is much less successful in accounting for short-term variations in the ongoing decisions of management, and the willingness to adapt to changes in the environment by altering budgetary allocations in the short run. This would suggest that there are additional factors which systematically influence decision-making but which we have not considered.

THE PROBLEM OF ADAPTATION

The weakness of the neo-Weberian model may result from deficiencies in our understanding of the process of organizational adaptation. The model assumes that when there is a discrepancy between performance and the exigencies of the environment, the organization adapts. Adaptation occurs through changes in the structure and the decision rules, changes in the preferences or goals of management, or changes in the management itself. Thus, the organization will adapt to changes in its environment and continue to function in a rational and appropriate way. In this sense, adaptation means successful change, not just change of an unknown type.

If organizations tend to persist in an established course of action despite changes in their size, revenues, and performance levels, our ability to account for differences in decision outcomes is greatly reduced. If the magnitude and timing of changes in decision outcomes respond to some variable that is not included in the model, the problem is compounded. Variations in the power of the model when applied to different industrial sectors may reflect the uneven distribution of that unknown factor.

The observation that organizations sometimes fail to adapt is hardly earth-shattering. There is a wealth of literature that casts doubt upon the smoothness and reliability of organizational adaptation. Ecology models of organization use the failure to adapt as a reason to reject rational theories of organization preferring instead to simply chart the frequency of organizational death (G. Carroll 1988a). But it may be more useful to consider the extent to which one can integrate non-rational factors into a broader framework.

Organizations often give the appearance of fragmented, polycentred, chaotic change (Cohen, March and Olsen 1972). Particularly when contracting, they are characterized by high levels of stress and conflict, the exiting of the most productive employees, and an increased centralization which often paralyses decision-making (Kolarska and Aldrich 1980; Levine 1980; Staw, Sundelands and Dutton 1981; Bozeman and Slusher 1979). The process of problemistic, biased search can lead to a cycle of disintegration in which the original problem is compounded by being ignored, the search for solutions is based upon an inaccurate conception of the problem, and solutions which do not alleviate the problem are followed. One method of dealing with the problem is used and then rationalized, a form of 'ex post hoc rationalization'; or the wrong search strategy is employed (Carter 1971; Cyert 1978; Dunbar and Goldberg 1978; Holsti 1978; Stout 1980).

There are two broad types of prescriptions for dealing with change and uncertainty. The first is the 'leap of faith', which often takes the form of a call for 'vision' or 'intuitive irrationality'. Like the 'Little engine that could', this type of solution assumes that once the organization (or its management) have decided on a course of action, it will be both correct and attainable. The second type puts its faith in planning, more commonly referred to as strategic action. Even Richard Cyert, one of the originators of the behavioural theory of problemistic, biased search, has himself come to view its longer run implications as prescriptive, and suggests that organizations should develop new perspectives to deal with the possibility of long-term problems (1978). Many popular management texts advocate better planning. One purports to teach managers how they can 'correctly define problems' and how to 'distinguish between simple and complex problems' (Kilmann 1989). But this assumes both knowledge and a willingness to act.

The process of adaptation, like these prescriptions for change, requires:

1   that managers can recognize the difference between problems which affect the viability of the organization and those which do not; and

2 that having made this distinction, they will take the correct action; or
3 they will recognize when they are not best able to solve the problem, and
  will then cede power to another group.

Alternatively, the model supposes that other stakeholders of the organization can make this distinction, despite the limitations on the information available to them, and that they can and will act to change the management before the viability of the organization is threatened.

These requirements for adaptation seem to be inconsistent with the rational model itself. In the first place, they rely upon either altruism or omniscience on the part of management; characteristics which are incompatible with the assumption of self-interest as the major motivation of management. Second, they do not reflect the slowness and the uncertainty of change in the preferences of managers themselves. Managers have cause–effect beliefs, or a 'prior ideology' (Child 1972), and ideology by definition does not change easily or quickly. These requirements also ignore the unwillingness of managers to address difficult problems for which solutions are not known or outcomes are uncertain. The tendency for organizations to be 'conservative' in their problem-solving has long been recognized and is consistent with both cognitive theories of uncertainty avoidance and studies of decision-making (Mack 1971). Organizations prefer to deal with familiar problems for which there are known solutions with predictable outcomes. But the requirements for adaptation necessitate another type of behaviour.

This failure to explain lack of adaptation seems to arise from three major problems, all of which follow from the assumption that 'management' can be homogeneous and rational. One is the assumption that the difference between the short term and the long term is clear, rather than accepting that the organization 'muddles along,' treating all problems as short-term problems. The second is that the model underestimates the constraining effect of structure on behaviour. Third, the general dilemma of 'who will guard the guardians?' has a more specific application: who can manage the managers, or replace them?

The 'nickel and dime' effect

Theories of decision-making indicate that uncertainty avoidance precludes decisions being made in anything but the short run, and it is not clear how a distinction between 'critical' and 'non-critical' problems can be made when management's perspective is the short term. When problems are always viewed in the short run, a 'nickel and dime' effect develops (Hage 1980). It is similar to the outcome problems associated with policy models of incrementalism in which a series of small decisions are made which eventually produce an outcome quite different from what was intended (Goodin and Waldner 1979; Braybrooke and Lindblom 1963).

Management texts and theoretical studies of decision-making often provide a matrix in which programmed, synoptic or rational decision-making is cited as the optimal method only when preferences are clear and uncertainty is low (Daft 1983; Stout 1980). This, unfortunately, is the least frequent case. Other types of decision calculi are required or prescribed for all other cases. But the problem is that organizations, by breaking big problems into little ones, or by acting 'as if' knowledge or agreement exists, do not change their patterns of decision-making. They continue to follow the prescription of programmed, synoptic, or rational decision-making, following the SORs in use in their own firm and, frequently, in firms across industries. Pfeffer has gone so far as to suggest that some theorists believe that '[t]o understand a given organization it is necessary and largely sufficient to understand these performance programs and procedures' (Pfeffer 1982: 235).

The effect of this process is that organizations act by following the pattern established when similar or relatively similar problems were experienced in the past. They institutionalize successes in problem definition, search or choice by incorporating them into their standard operating procedures. As each problem is handled sequentially, the adjustment process is hampered by an inability to detect the cumulative effect of this series of small decisions. Past successes can be transformed into current errors by a failure to recognize that adaptation is required.

The impact of structure

We have seen how organizational structure and, in particular, the size of the administrative component, varies with the function and size of the organization. The administrative component is larger for organizations operating in a complex environment with a complex technology, but this does not explain the wide variation among organizations of the same type. Generally, as organizations become larger, or older, they are more likely to be complex and to be run by managers whose primary concern is co-ordination. These types of organization are also more likely to be run by 'hired' managers whose 'best interests' lie in the direction of organizational control and survival. The resultant increase in administrative costs could be the result of a tendency for the managerial sub-system to dominate larger, older, or more complex organizations. Thus a greater emphasis would be placed upon administrative activities as size and age increase, not simply because of size and age but also as a consequence of the management type, a variable which is exogenous to the model.

In successful organizations structure, performance and outcomes are functions of adapting to contextual and structural factors, and the 'correct' goals of the management. In the short term, management designs the structure of the organization to fit their perception of the contingent variables, and in the longer term structure should adjust to the extent that the contingency factors change and are recognized to change.

The last phrase, 'are recognized to change', may point to a central problem. The structure of the organization is intended to provide it with stability. But this stability is achieved by the filtering of information, and by the reinforcement of existing patterns of behaviour. These are the characteristics which led one author to refer to management as 'prisoners rather than managers' of the structure of the organization (Theonig and Friedberg 1976: 314). The filtering role of the structure limits the ability of management to perceive changes in the environment independently of the existing structure. This, coupled with the preference for uncertainty avoidance on the part of the organization and its members, will tend to keep the structure of the organization intact. Thus the structure, while acting as a stabilizing influence, not only constrains the organization in the short run, but constrains the ability of *those in control* to recognize changes in the environment, and to bring about adaptation and a change in outcomes.

Management, adaptation, and change

Given the power of the management group, the characteristics of the senior managers are important independent variables in considering the way in which organizations decide, and in attempting to explain their outcomes. The existing literature does provide evidence of differences in behaviour between organizations based upon variations or changes in their management. It would appear from these studies that in terms of resource allocation and outcomes, owner-managers behave differently from professional-managers; that a powerful ideology or powerful group within the management can affect outcomes; that bureaucratic organizations protect administrative costs in times of declining resources and favour them when resources are not scarce; that changing the management may change administrative costs; and, finally, that changing the management sometimes affects performance, and sometimes it does not (Amihud *et al.* 1983; M. Brown 1982; Lawriwsky 1984).

Managers obtain their positions through successful bargaining and retain their power by resisting pressure from other groups. It seems likely that they will act to maintain their position by defining problems as being within their own sphere of knowledge, and will limit access to information and to the 'inner group'. If forced to cede power to others because the future of the organization is at stake, they may try to replace themselves with new members who have similar values and expertise, thus retarding the adaptation of the organization (Allen and Panian 1982; Michels 1966; Pettigrew 1973).

In the long term the structure of the organization is supposed to change because the knowledge or values of those directing it have changed. A more reasonable expectation is that change will occur when the management itself changes, and new members bring new values and knowledge. This final requirement for adaptation may be the one most frequently met. That is, some group external to management acts to replace the management. Starbuck *et al.* (1978) suggests that the easiest and most effective way to bring a new perspective into an organization is to change the top three levels of management. Janowitz's (1960) classic study provides an example of this as a method used to produce change in the US Army. The White House, which had been a relatively inactive part of the organizational coalition, became active and intervened to break the existing pattern of behaviour by changing the type of individuals selected for Chief of Staff and other senior positions. Similarly, studies of administrative change in Britain during the Thatcher era suggest this may be the most effective means of achieving organizational adaptation in public enterprises (Common *et al.* 1992).

In order to bring about this change, some external group – a previously passive part of the organization – must take action. But by definition passive groups normally have demands which can be easily met, and when they become dissatisfied or their demands are not being met, the costs to them of obtaining information and taking action are high (Adrien and Press 1968). Lawriwsky (1984: 50–1) explains why stockholders do not sell their shares when performance declines by pointing out the high costs of taking action for such passive or weak groups. In cases of very poor performance or high levels of dissatisfaction, it is likely that they will exit from the organization, rather than forcing adaptation upon it (Hirschman 1970). Nurses may exit from their profession rather than striking or taking other action which would force a restructuring of the health care coalition. Dissatisfied automobile purchasers may switch to imports. Faculty members who are faced with declining research facilities and increasing class sizes may leave the university, take early retirement, or (if tenured) simply cease to carry out research and switch to computer-scored examinations – a form of exit. All of these are cases in which passive sectors of organizations exit instead of forcing change.

Within the literature of political science it has become a truism that, if one wishes to achieve change, it is necessary 'to throw the rascals out', to replace the party in power with another party, one which is demonstrably different from the existing government in its policies and values. Changing the leader is rarely sufficient. To use a somewhat mundane example, the municipal reform movements in Canada in the late 1970s were successful only in cases where the majority of the council and the senior administration, and not the mayor alone, were replaced (Higgins 1986). But politics also provides an example of why changing managers may not work – if those coming in are essentially the same. In such cases changing the top two or three levels of the hierarchy will have little effect. Exchanging one middle-of-the-road political party for another may not produce anything but an inexperienced cabinet.

Most organizations may be able to successfully adapt to environmental changes during periods of growth. Ultimately, under 'norms of rationality' the dominant coalition within the organization will reform to include those parts of the organization most knowledgeable of, or with the most experience of, the problem at hand. The coalition will change (or be changed) to meet the needs of the organization.

Unfortunately, this may not happen until the organization has reached a point at which recovery is no longer possible. In two recent widely publicized cases, the failure of Campeau Corporation and Olympia and York Developments, it was their bankers which eventually took action, but at a time when it was too late to ensure the viability of the organization. When times are bad and the organization faces a period of decline, adaptation becomes more difficult. And yet, it is during such periods that adaptation by changing the composition of the dominant coalition is most essential for the continued viability of the organization. In times of crisis the question becomes not whether organizations will adapt given sufficient time, but what factors can impede the rate of change so that adaptation may no longer be a relevant alternative.

CONCLUSION

The expectation of adaptation is one of the weakest aspects of the neo-Weberian model because it ignores considerable evidence of organizational rigidity, and of persisting states of turmoil, in response to pressure for change. It is unrealistic to assume that organizations, as simply a collectivity of individuals, can or will distinguish long-term, critical threats from short-term normal problems. It underestimates the power of organizational structures to inhibit change. Ultimately, it may expect and require the impossible of those who manage organizations. It is management who must be capable of recognizing critical problems; it is they who must be willing and able to bring about appropriate structural changes; and it is they who must cede power to others if their own talents are inappropriate to the problems at hand.

It is a reasonable assumption that the people who manage large organizations tend to be unusually capable men and women. In some cases, then, they may be able to meet these extraordinary expectations. In other cases an external group will have the ability and the will to replace the existing management, despite the many advantages of incumbency. Those organizations will adapt to environmental change much as the neo-Weberian model predicts. In many other cases, however, organizational adaptation will be resisted and delayed. When change occurs, it will respond to factors other than norms of rationality. Inappropriate responses will be implemented. The performance level of the organization will be depressed. In extreme cases, and especially in the face of a particularly hostile environment, the organization may not survive.

In the years since 1982 some firms in the study (such as Cadillac-Fairview Corporation) have experienced growth and success. Others (such as the Continental Illinois Bank and many of the savings and loan companies) have experienced spectacular failure. Some (such as Campeau Corporation) have experienced both conditions, euphoric success followed by equally dramatic failure. Many of the firms studied have disappeared completely. These problems were not limited to firms within any one industry group. Is there some systematic factor which can account for the differences in the ability of these firms to adapt, thereby explaining variations in their subsequent performance levels?

In the next chapter I argue that this failure of organizations to adapt may be explained in part by the existence within the organization of systematic bias. 'Bias', in this context, is simply a label for the category of behaviour which Talcott Parsons described more formally as a 'systematic divergence from the rational norm' (1949: 702). There is considerable theoretical and empirical evidence which indicates that individuals are biased in their perceptions of situations, and in the decisions they make. What is not clear, however, is the extent to which the natural tendency for individuals to be biased can produce a bias in the actual decisions of an organization. Nor do we know the extent to which this organizational bias can affect the outcomes of the organization over time. It is reasonable to suppose, however, that if there is a bias in day-to-day decision-making that is not corrected through the processes of organizational adaptation, its persistence will eventually bias the performance and outcomes of the organization.

I will show that a revision to the basic model which incorporates systematic bias in the forms of management type and systemic values can explain differences in decision-making and performance among firms. In particular, the obstacles to adaptation which I have discussed – the constraining effect of structure, the tendency of management to replace itself with similar people, and the managerial inclination to treat most decisions in an incremental fashion – all act to reinforce the 'biases of management'. This is not to say that the structural and contextual circumstances of the organization are unimportant in determining action; we have seen that the extent of technological determinism is high. But national culture and management type also influence the factors that are considered in resource allocation decisions, and affect the overall performance of the organization.

In the next three chapters, two specific possibilities are considered. In the case of systemic bias, there are specific cultural values shared by most of the members of an organization. These values can inhibit organizational action by eliminating from consideration alternatives with which they conflict. For example, in countries in which tenure or 'employment for life' is a deeply entrenched cultural value, firing employees who are un-productive may not be considered. The second possibility, managerial bias, arises when the key managers within the organization share a common orientation, derived from factors such as education or internal corporate culture, which precludes them from considering certain alternatives. An organization in which all or most of the senior management have been trained in finance, for example, will tend to define problems and make decisions differently from one in which all or most of the senior manage-ment have been trained as engineers. The first part of this study, therefore, attempts to measure the extent to which the decision-making processes of organizations are biased towards outcomes consistent with cultural values and/or managerial orientation.

The analysis will initially focus on two common management types within private sector organizations in North America; those whose senior managers are drawn primarily from the technical or production sections of the organization, and those whose senior managers are drawn primarily from the managerial or co-ordination and control sections. We will see that firms in similar task environments facing similar problems over a number of years, respond and perform differently, depending upon whether they are run by technical managers who are likely to be oriented towards pro-duction, or by administrative managers who typically place more emphasis upon control. While individual values and experience are relevant and recognized aspects of organizational action, existing theories less often consider cases in which the structure and management of the organization are such that individual values unintentionally become both collective and predictable. When this happens, the resulting organizational bias can help to explain and predict otherwise inexplicable organizational action.

This study is not an attempt to track the internal decision paths or individual cognitive processes within the organization or management group itself, nor to untangle internal power relationships. The initial empirical test is limited to a small sample of firms to ensure that the expectation of bias can be supported through external, objective measures. The more general application of the findings and, in particular the relationship between sub-system representation and performance are then considered through a study of a broader range of firms and industry sectors.

In changing environments there is frequently a call for some new type of manager. 'Now we need order, next we need change and then we need to control our destiny' (Czarnlawska-Joerges and Wolff 1991: 541) In the 1990s, with a new environment, there is an increasing call for yet another new type of manager – one who can cope with an economic and social turbulence. But it may be more productive to consider if there are ways to structure organizations such that we are not always playing 'catch up' in an environment which has already changed.

Recognition of the systematic impact of organizational bias may be important in explaining why organizations act as they do, and why there are differing levels of performance among them. This is not to say that bias is always bad. Organizational bias may have some benefits. The entire movement expounding and explaining the virtues of internal corporate cultures, for example, is an attempt at institutionalizing a bias considered to be positive. But the bias must be recognized as such. Since one of its effects is to reduce the ability of the organization and management to recognize or correct errors, an organization that is influenced by an unacknowledged bias may limp along, a victim of the behaviour that Parkinson called 'injelititis' or 'palsied paralysis'. In such organizations, change may take place only in the face of a severe environmental jolt, if it occurs at all.

Organizational bias often persists even when shortcomings have been recognized. The cartoon character, Pogo, proclaimed, 'We have seen the enemy, and he is us!' Few managers are inclined to follow this sage example. Instead, they are likely to assume that unsatisfactory performance is a consequence of inadequacies in other parts of the organization, or to attribute the problem entirely to the hostile character of the environment. Even if the managers are replaced, a failure to look beyond the symptom of poor performance to the underlying problem of organizational bias makes it unlikely that there will be a conscious attempt to alter the management type. In some cases the organization may have the good fortune to experience an appropriate (although inadvertent) change in management type. In others the type of management, and thus the type of bias, will persist despite the change in the actual managers.

The prescriptive literature frequently require managers to behave in ways that are uncharacteristic because they are incongruent with deeply seated biases that the managers share. These prescriptions are then filtered and distorted by the bias of the organization as its managers attempt to implement them. A new management technique that is incongruent with the values and norms of those who must implement it, whether these values and norms are a product of the systemic or internal cultures of the organization, is almost certainly doomed to failure.

This book differs from standard management texts which attempt to teach or exhort managers to behave in particular ways. Instead, it accepts that certain types of managers, certain types of organizations and more importantly, certain forms of management configurations, will behave in a predictable, patterned fashion. Sometimes the bias of the organization is positive or neutral in its effects on performance; sometimes it is negative; and occasionally it is a recipe for disaster. Seldom, however, will it be possible for those who manage the organization and share its bias to change this fundamental behavioural tendency. But to the extent that organizational bias is a predictable, structural characteristic of the organization, it is also amenable to structural correction. I will suggest three ways organizations can be structured or changed to adjust for organizational bias. In cases in which groups external to the organization have the power to replace its management, these prescriptions may be of value. And when no such external force exists, we at least have a better understanding of why some organizations fail in circumstances in which other, apparently similar, organizations succeed.

2 The notion of bias

INTRODUCTION

In the last chapter we discussed one of the continuing problems of organization theory – the inability to explain why organizations sometimes fail to adapt. The problem, it should be noted, is not that organizations do not alter their decisions. Changes in the decision patterns are relatively common. The difficulty is that these changes do not correspond in a rational way to changes in the structural and contextual variables. Michael Porter (1985) has suggested that, in order to succeed, organizations must adjust or adapt their basic goals. In the last chapter I suggested why this does not occur. In this chapter we consider why, even when change occurs, an inappropriate solution may be chosen. This is done by developing more fully the concept of organizational bias as an additional non-rational factor that is not adequately recognized in the literature, and which may help to explain systematic variations in decisions across organizations.

Both the sources of bias and the conditions under which it can affect the outcomes of the organization are found in most, if not all, organizations. The components of organizational bias are not newly discovered phenomena, but by drawing together a number of types of behaviour which have been recognized in the literature, we increase our ability to see them as related factors which have a common impact upon organizations. The similarity is that they all tend to affect the decision-making process of the organization in a non-rational manner, and thus give the impression of organizations behaving in unique, unpredictable ways.

BIAS IN ORGANIZATIONS

Before going further, it is necessary to distinguish among rational, non-rational and irrational action. Although the terms are widely used, they do not have generally accepted meanings which are suitable for empirical research (Bryman 1984; Shrwastava *et al.* 1987). For my purposes, rational actions are those 'which can be logically linked to an end, not only in respect to the person performing them but also to those other people who have more extensive knowledge'.[1] In terms of organizational behaviour, then, rational behaviour is behaviour which can be understood and duplicated by other organizations with the same knowledge. Non-rational action is behaviour which can be predicted and understood because it follows a pattern, but a pattern which can be recognized only if we have additional knowledge of the problem or the organization – knowledge which is not logically linked to the apparent end. Irrational behaviour is action which appears perverse or illogical, which follows no discernible pattern, which is not logically linked to any apparent end, and which thus cannot be understood.

Anyone familiar with organizations can provide examples of actions which do not appear to be rational. In an attempt to explain such behaviour Starbuck *et al.* (1978) refer to organizations with a suicide wish, and Cyert (1978) uses the phrase, a 'vicious circle of disintegration'. Dunleavy (1981) writes of a problem cycle, and Stout discusses 'the consequences of a failure to acknowledge errors' (1980: 128). In each case, the authors are referring to organizations which fail to adapt.

A number of explanations have been offered for observations such as these. One is that different managerial styles produce different outcomes (Ford 1981). A second is that different structures limit the information and flexibility of the organization to varying degrees, but this does not explain why the differences in structure exist. It has also been suggested that organizations in fact have different but unstated goals (Perrow 1970), differing power structures (Abell 1975; Pettigrew 1973), different 'institutionalized myths' (Meyer and Rowan 1977), or different 'established stereotypes' (Wilensky 1969). These explanations, while accounting for differences in behaviour, managerial style, and structure, do so by considering them to be functions of some intent which is unknown. Mintzberg (1983) takes this further by differentiating between organizations on the basis of whether the goal of the organization is to achieve its ostensible mission, or to do something else as determined by those in control of the organization. There is also a large body of literature which distinguishes between organizations managed by their owners and those run by hired professionals, pointing to differences in the motivations of the two types of managers (Lawriwsky 1984). We are still left with the problem of explaining specific differences in behaviour among organizations that are managed by non-owners, and which are otherwise relatively similar.

One solution is simply to conclude that some organizations do not behave in a rational fashion. They are irrational or perverse; the means–ends calculus is out of tune with reality (Landau 1973). Another is to accept the apparently idiosyncratic nature of managers as an unavoidable fact of life; one which may be manifest in the not uncommon refrain that 'you cannot understand this organization if you have not been here twenty years, and knew "old Gordon" who retired in 1958'. Yet another is to view organizational behaviour in terms of statistical probabilities – there are x possible sources of a problem and y means of defining the problem. The odds of correctly identifying and solving a problem then become a matter of random chance (Cohen, March and Olsen 1972). To the extent that any of these positions is valid, organizational behaviour must remain unpredictable.

A final possibility is that some part of the decision process is non-rational. In other words, the decision calculus follows a predictable, patterned response, but it is based upon some factor other than the exigencies of the current problem. If we can identify that factor, our ability to explain and predict the decisions of organizations will improve.

The rational model has come under heavy fire in recent years as it has become clear that 'the conditions under which decisions are reached in organizations are too complex to meet the criteria of rationality' (Morgan 1990: 64). There have, also, been a number of alternatives offered to it as the dominant model. One approach is to throw up your hands and accept the basic paradox exemplified by the garbage can model (Cohen, March and Olsen 1972). A second is based upon history and the study of institutions (Meyer and Rowan 1977). A third is concerned with power and the ecology of organizations (G. Carroll 1988; Morgan 1990; Pfeffer and Salancik 1978; Pettigrew 1973). As Bryman (1984) points out, however, they all depend to some extent upon assumptions about the internal processes within organizations, and they tend to differ in their conceptions and definitions of individual and organizational level rationality. One recent book offers fourteen different alternatives to the rational model, but none of these approaches attempts to build non-rational action into the existing rational model in a systematic fashion which would allow explanation and prediction of organizational action (Czarniawska-Joerges 1992; Zey 1992). I hope to do just that.

Considered individually, non-rational action and irrational action may be indistinguishable. In both cases the central characteristic is the lack of an obvious connection between the action and any known goal of the organization. The key to distinguishing non-rational behaviour is the discovery of a persistent pattern of activity that is common to certain organizations which also share characteristics within their management group which could logically produce this departure from the rational norm. Characteristics which have this effect create an *organizational bias* towards specific actions or outcomes. If outcomes continue to be biased in a given direction, over time they will alter the performance level of the organization.

What is 'organizational bias'?

'Bias' is an odd word, one which has a pejorative meaning for most people. Statisticians go to great lengths to assume it away, and management texts warn against it. The only context in which it seems to have a positive meaning is dress-making.

Individual bias, however, is simply a patterned, predictable preference for a certain outcome or state of affairs, arising from the individual's values, experience and knowledge. It is, in effect, a way of shortening the decision-making process for individuals. If you have a bias against fast food restaurants based upon a preference for sitting at tables and your unpleasant past experience with the local hot dog stand, the decision about which restaurant to go to can be taken more quickly – all fast food outlets can be avoided. Thus bias is a common and important, but non-rational, aspect of decision making.

But bias has another aspect. To the extent that it provides a short cut, or a patterned divergence from the 'rational norm', its effect is to inhibit consideration of information which does not conform to these preferences. You may ignore the fact that a new fast food restaurant provides tables and serves steak rather than hot dogs. Nevertheless, because bias is patterned, when it is recognized to exist, its effects can be predicted.

The term 'organizational bias' is used here in a way analogous to its use in statistics. In statistics, biased estimators result if the assumption of a 'normal' population is violated, or if some unmeasured variable outside of the model acts to distort the predicted outcomes.[2] Similarly, organizational bias results when some factor not logically related to the problem at hand acts to distort or skew the decision outcomes of the organization in a systematic fashion. Knowledge of the existence and form of bias within an organization can thus be of help in understanding differences between organizations, and in explaining behaviour which, superficially at least, appears to be irrational or perverse. Such knowledge may permit us to predict non-rational aspects of the behaviour of organizations.

References to bias are sometimes found in the literature about organizations. I have never found it defined or measured in any specific way. Usually it is invoked as an explanation for individual action. Yet one reason for the existence of formal structures in organizations is to control and restrict the effect of the various biases held by individuals within the organization. Non-rational preferences can affect an organization's outcomes and performance only if they represent widely held values shared by virtually all members of the organization, or by all of the members of its powerful core – the management.

Widely held values that are not intrinsic to the model of rational action could have this effect. We assume that the members of an organization collectively value the ostensible, manifest goals of their organization, be they profit, the provision of a service or whatever. If some other unstated value is so important as to cause a decline in the achievement of the manifest goals, we have organizational bias. Similarly, if a particular means is valued more highly than the manifest goals, organizational bias can take the form of goal displacement.

The goal of Dofasco, a Canadian steel manufacturer, is to make profits by producing steel. Its slogan is 'our strength is people'. If concern for the employees were to intrude to the point that steel production is reduced, organizational bias would exist. When a bank, the First Chicago Corporation, pursues a policy of 'relationship management' by staffing nine new administrative divisions, despite a 40 per cent decline in profits, organizational bias may be responsible. When a mortgage company, London Life, would not lend funds for the purchase of condominiums during a period when condominiums accounted for 40 per cent of the new housing market, and based this policy on the fact that the senior executives 'did not like condos' (Cartwright and Wekerle 1978), organizational bias seems a probable diagnosis. (In the latter case, the bias was beneficial since the market for condominiums collapsed shortly afterwards.)

In the sense used here, then, 'non-rational' approximates the Weberian concept of substantive rationality, and Simon's (1965) definition of 'subjective rationality', for it is only predictable and can only be logically understood by inclusion of knowledge about factors such as values and experience. The goal is to classify and predict those elements described as 'something else'; to find factors common to many organizations which create patterns of non-rational behaviour, thus making such behaviour predictable. In addition to its explanatory value, this exercise should also contribute to prescriptive theory. It is not enough simply to prescribe a change in organizational culture, or ideology, or even management, any of which might or might not alter the biases of the organization. It is first necessary to understand the consequences of the current biases, in order to assess the probable effects of the prescribed change.

THE SOURCES OF BIAS

The literature on organizations identifies four types of values, or biases, which might affect the behaviour of individuals. These are cognitive bias, self-interest bias, technical or managerial bias and systemic bias. Cognitive and self-interest bias are incorporated in the neo-Weberian model, and their effects are either counterbalanced by the off-setting biases of other members of the organization, or they can be controlled by aspects of the organizational design that the model prescribes (Cyert and March 1963;

Downs 1967). They are similar in that they are both psychologically or individually based, and in that they are subjective and cannot be eliminated. Cognitive and self-interest bias are part of what might tritely be termed the 'human condition'. They have been studied extensively, and their effects are well-documented (Downing and Brady 1979; March and Simon 1958; Lord, Leper and Strack 1975).

Cognitive bias is simply the preference of individuals for certainty. It is a preference for the known over the unknown, and for the reduction of search costs by considering only limited, known alternatives. It is fine to tell managers that they must learn to 'manage paradoxes' or learn to 'live in sand castles' (Peters 1986; Hedburg *et al.* 1976). But it is likely that they will also unlearn this behaviour quickly. The paradox will disappear at the first sign of a panacea to resolve it and the castles will develop solid walls. The effect of cognitive bias has been well developed, and is an accepted part of management and organizational theory (Pfeffer 1982: 233–6). This is the form of bias that is central to Simon's 'cognitive limits to rationality', and it forms the basis of decision theory. The predilection of managers for 'one best way', prescriptive theories – or five best ways, or seven best ways – may be a reflection of cognitive bias (Mintzberg 1979; Peters and Waterman 1982).

Much of the power dynamic within organizations can be seen as an exercise in self-interest.[3] '[T]he logic of self-interest requires that managers operate the firm in their self-interest', according to Williamson (1963: 239), and 'their effective control insures that this objective will be pursued.' Nevertheless, self-interest bias does not normally have a long-term effect upon the organization for, as Downs (1967) has pointed out, it can be overcome by widening the group of decision-makers to the point that no one individual's self-interest can dominate. Any organization which has a form of bargaining for perquisites or resources can counteract the effect of self-interest bias.

The neo-Weberian model recognizes both cognitive preferences and self-interest as sources of bias at the individual level, then, and it provides prescriptive remedies to prevent these types of bias from affecting outcomes and performance. The model does not deal as adequately with the two remaining sources of bias – technical background and cultural values.

Simon deals primarily with individual, cognitive bias and its effect in limiting the rationality of individuals, but he considers it to be subsumed within the rationality of the organization.

> [T]he term 'rational behavior', as employed here, refers to rationality when that behavior is evaluated in terms of the objectives of the larger organization; . . . the difference in direction of the individual's aims

from those of the larger organization is just one of those elements of nonrationality with which the theory must deal.

(1965: 41)

Moreover, Simon does not seem to think that this is a problem within the management or 'controlling group' of the organization, 'whose personal values may be of various kinds, but who assume the responsibility of maintaining the life of the organization in order that they may attain these values' (1965: 122).

Simon also recognized the existence of 'technical bias' in that the education and, more particularly, the organizational experience of individuals affect their definitions of problems and their choices. Certainly, in hiring most professionals we are hiring them *for* their technical bias; we assume they have some set of values and training which will influence their decision-making. Concern arises when these professionals apply their biases to the management of the organizations. Child (1972) recognizes the existence of managerial bias in his discussion of 'managerial ideology' as a prior condition for the establishment of an organization's 'domain', and its relationship to technology and the environment.

Cyert and March recognized bias with respect to choice, communication within the organization, and search processes. 'Bias from prior experience or training is implicit in our assumptions of search learning, local specialization in problem solving and subunit goal differentiation' (1963: 122). They deal with bias in choice only to the extent of recognizing that it exists, and that it varies 'for a variety of reasons' between organizations. They assume that for almost every instance of bias there is bias correction:

[B]ias can be substantially ignored in our models except under conditions where the internal biases in the firm are all (or substantially all) in one direction or where biases in one direction are located in part of the organization with an extremely favourable balance of power.

(Cyert and March 1963: 122)

My point is simply that it cannot be ignored. This condition for bias will exist in most, if not all, organizations. In much of the literature, particularly the management literature, there is an assumption that managers or management can be, or can be taught to be, rational or right. This is exemplified in the comment: 'People can be taught to be better leaders . . . just like they can be taught to be better golfers' (Business International 1987: 16). In the same vein Sutherland suggests that the problem of many managers is that they are not intellectually competent to manage because they are not rational enough, and devotes the remainder of a lengthy book to correcting that situation by 'expanding the boundaries of rationality'

(1977: 7). Mintzberg treats management as one individual, the Chief Executive Officer, who 'may not know everything, but he typically knows more than anyone else' (1983: 122).

Although the idea that managers are omniscient is slowly losing ground, there is still an assumption that (with a little help from a management consultant) they may be able to consider all the 'relevant' aspects of a problem. 'How to' management books invariably provide a checklist of steps to be taken even if some of them – tribal practices, the art of Zen, astrology, magic – seem less than rational themselves. More constructively, Bennis and Nanus suggest that 'the leaders select, organize, structure and interpret information about the future in an attempt to construct a viable and credible vision' (1985: 100). To the extent that the goals of the organization are set by the management; and their actions are logically connected in some way to these goals; and the management group has knowledge and experience of all aspects of the organization's task environment; this is no doubt a viable prescription.

The role of management is important in understanding the problem of adaptation, or lack of adaptation, in organizations. In the last chapter, we saw that the potential for overcoming each of the three main obstacles to organizational adaptation depends very heavily upon the omniscience, the rationality, and the altruism of management. Management must be able to distinguish between critical long-term threats to the organization and normal short-term problems if they are to avoid the 'nickel and dime effect'. Their perspective must extend beyond the boundaries of the existing organizational structure if they are to be able to perceive and act upon the need for structural change. And they must perceive their own deficiencies and be willing to cede power to others when circumstances so demand.

Despite the heroic dimensions of the role assigned to management by the model, the managers of some organizations seem to come reasonably close to meeting these requirements. In those cases, the behaviour of the organization roughly matches the predictions of the model, and when the external environment changes the organization adapts in an appropriate manner. Of the firms within this study, Cadillac-Fairview Corporation came closest to matching this ideal – at various points it changed its structure, management type (and managers), and its organizational domain, in order to adapt to shifts in its environment. In some other cases in which organizations behave in apparently irrational ways, or fail to adapt to environmental changes, the departure from the model undoubtedly is idiosyncratic or random. Our interest, however, lies with the remaining and substantial category in which organizational behaviour departs from the neo-Weberian model, but in ways which are patterned and predictable. The source of these patterned departures from the rational norm may be an organizational bias of one of the two types that are not included in the model – managerial and systemic bias.

Managerial bias

We have suggested that the composition of the management group is representative of some combination of the institutional, managerial and technical sub-systems of the organization. As Katz and Kahn have pointed out:

> the top decision-making group is limited by the values and expertise of the sub-system in which they are trained; for example the engineering point of view of the former head of the production department will vary from the market orientation of the former head of sales.
>
> (Katz and Kahn 1978: 499)

If all or most sub-systems are represented in that top decision-making group, and if the distribution of power among representatives of different sub-systems is relatively equitable, these individual biases should cancel each other out. The only consequence for the organization will be the benefit it gains as a result of the diversity of experiences of its senior managers.

The situation is quite different, however, if a single sub-system has a dominant role in the management of the organization. Those responsible for making vital decisions will be familiar, in such cases, with only a limited portion of the activities of the organization. Search and decision-making are likely to be biased, outcomes may be skewed, and the organization's ability to adapt to environmental changes probably will be inhibited by the inability of its management to 'see the whole'. This type of phenomenon is what Dunleavy (1981) has labelled a 'technical ideology' – a set of professional beliefs and values which is sufficiently strong to colour the outcomes of the organization even after new knowledge should have indicated that those values and professional solutions are no longer appropriate. Managerial bias often leads the manager to 'feel' that he understands the future when, in fact, he does not (March and Shapira 1992); to act 'as if' he has knowledge when, in fact, he does not.

Nor is such a situation likely to be self-correcting. Few managers are likely to be sufficiently knowledgeable and objective to recognize situations in which their own shortcomings are responsible for the problems of the organization. Fewer still are likely to be so altruistic that, having come to this disheartening conclusion, they voluntarily pass the reins of power to others. In some cases, of course, other parties will have the power to displace the existing management, but the problem may result from the *type* of management rather than the abilities of the individuals. In the absence of an understanding of managerial types and managerial bias, such a change may well alter the personnel without affecting the bias.

Managerial bias – that is, a bias resulting from the dominance of any one sub-system – can affect both the short-term outcomes of the organization, then, and its longer term performance. And it should be noted that managerial bias is a common phenomenon. The literature on managerial succession tells us that managers tend to select and promote people similar to themselves (Pfeffer and Salancik 1978: 236–7). As Barnard pointed out half a century ago, a 'formal and orderly conception of the whole is rarely present, perhaps even rarely possible, except to a few men of executive genius, or a few executive organizations the personnel of which is comprehensively sensitive and well integrated' (1938: 239). In the absence of rare men of genius or management groups that are unusually comprehensive and sensitive, we find dominance by a single type of management, and the managerial bias that results.

In this study, I initially emphasize two managerial types that are common in private-sector organizations in North America; those dominated by representatives of the administrative sub-system, and those dominated by representatives of the technical sub-system. In a general sense, technical dominance can be illustrated by the firms in the auto industry in its early years, which were dominated by production men (Halberstram 1986); the real estate development industry after the Second World War, which was dominated by engineers (Goldenberg 1981); the dominance of managers with a production background in the American steel industry (Strich 1986); and even by the image of bankers as a breed apart, inculcated with the norms of their profession (Sampson 1981). Administrative dominance is illustrated by the phenomenon of the MBA as a management generalist, and the 'professionalization' of administration.

Systemic bias

Cultural or systemic values are those values and beliefs held by groups or societies which constitute a common culture; it is these values which differentiate one culture from another and set the parameters of their institutions and political systems. Because these values are held by most of the individuals within a society, they are also held by most or all of the people within organizations in that society, and thus act to differentiate organizations in one culture from those in another. As Hofstede has argued:

> If perceptions of uncertainty are affected by personality variables, it is more than likely that they will also be affected by cultural variables. If different societies deal with uncertainty in different ways, this should affect the ways in which they build organizations to react to uncertainty.
> (Hofstede 1980: 57)

To the extent that organizations are constrained in their actions by such values, they would constitute a cultural or systemic source of organizational bias.

Cultural values shape the assumptions of all participants in the organization, including the management, about choices, search and the decision rules which are acceptable (Lammers and Hickson 1979: 403). They affect the definition of the problem and the consideration of alternative responses, with those alternatives which are inconsistent with cultural values being rejected or, more probably, not being considered at all. While a shared culture makes it easier for organizations to operate by providing a common, known set of standards, it can also limit the flexibility and adaptability of the organization. To the extent that a culture emphasizes values which have a high salience for organizational decision-making – values such as risk-taking or individualism, for example – these also are likely to colour all stages of the decision-making process. While most people, particularly those who have worked with members of another culture, or in another culture, intuitively accept the existence of systemic bias, there has been only limited progress made in measuring its effects.

Another well-established consequence of systemic bias is found in the structural characteristics of organizations. Pfeffer summarizes this when he states that 'there are certain employment practices and organizational arrangements that come to be culturally accepted and defined as good' (1982: 251). We know, for example, that the relationships among size, the centralization of decision-making and the degree of hierarchy, vary across cultural groups. This relationship between structure and culture has been studied and summarized extensively, yielding an impressive body of empirical information.[4]

The effects of systemic bias are also likely to persist in the longer term, thus distorting outcomes, because there is no strong countervailing set of values within the organization, and because the example provided by other organizations within the society is likely to be based on the same set of cultural values. Even if the systemic bias has negative consequences for the organization, corrective and adaptive processes may be inadequate because cultural values are often unquestioned, unconscious, and almost instinctive for members of a culture.

If an organization consciously attempts to adopt new techniques from another culture, these techniques are likely to be unintentionally altered by the dominant mind-set of the importing culture. Hofstede (1980: 381–3) makes this point well when he shows how Management by Objectives, at the time when it was sweeping the management scene, was transformed to suit the cultural values of each society into which it was introduced. Merkle's (1980) study of the development of Scientific Management produces a similar finding.

This type of systemic variation has been dealt with at great length in studies by political scientists of national administrative elites, where differences in outcomes (policy) and government management have been attributed to systemic differences in the values, patterns of training and norms of succession of senior bureaucrats (Aberbach *et al.* 1980; Carroll 1990c; Derlien 1992). It will become of increasing importance within the private sector as more firms deal in an international setting.

THE REVISED MODEL

The model outlined and tested in Chapter 1 included an unknown factor – managerial values and preferences – which was unique to each organization. Managers of similar organizations operating within similar environments should have similar goals and preferences, and – once the effects of the other variables have been taken into account – they should make similar decisions. Departures from this norm are expected to be limited in scope and relatively uncommon. To the extent that such departures do occur, the neo-Weberian model treats them as idiosyncratic, irrational, random and hence unpredictable. The revised model adds more definition to this amorphous factor by adding systemic values and the type of management that controls the organization, as preceding, non-rational variables which affect and bias the decisions of the organization. Thus, it attributes much of this previously unexplained behaviour not to irrationality or idiosyncratic preferences, but to non-rational but predictable biases.

These biases are held to have systematic effects on the actions of organizations, creating predictable patterns in their behaviour. If we distinguish cultures on the basis of systemic values that have a strong relevance to organizational behaviour, this knowledge should improve our ability to predict the decisions that organizations within those cultures will make. If we further distinguish among organizations on the basis of the sub-systems represented in their management groups, this also should increase the accuracy with which we can forecast or explain the decisions taken by the managers of those organizations.

One of the most difficult tasks facing an organization is to develop a clear perception of the nature or cause of a problem (Landau 1972). Organizations may fail to deal with a problem in terms of the known facts and outcome preferences. They act 'as if' they have knowledge or agreement which actually are lacking, and they do not learn from this error. Essentially, the problem you perceive, the alternatives you choose to evaluate and the choice you eventually make, are to a large extent a function of what you expect to see.

As Mannheim (1936) pointed out, and empirical studies have shown, impartiality in problem definition is uncommon (Alexis and Wilson 1967). In problem definition facts are very tenuous; the cause of a problem is almost impossible to determine objectively. The supposed cause of a

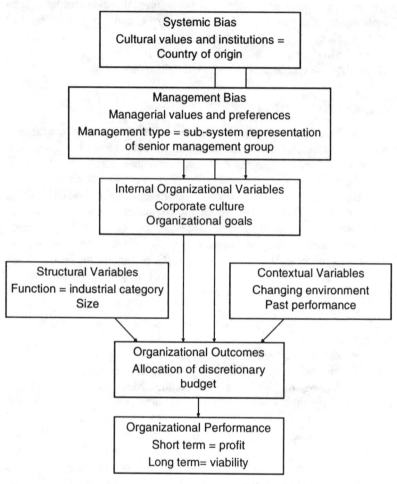

Figure 2.1 The revised model

problem is dependent upon those who define it, and the factual premises are, therefore, inextricably linked with the values of those defining the problem. It is a reasonable bet that the executive who said:

> Every part of the enterprise – every function, every department, every expenditure – must be evaluated in such terms as: how does this activity contribute to increased sales? how will this job help serve customers better? will this expenditure be one that customers are willing to pay for?
>
> (Business International 1987: 18)

came from a sales background not one concerned with profit margins and the bottom line. Dearborn and Simon (1958) demonstrated thirty-five years ago that accountants see and solve accounting problems, and salesmen see and solve sales problems – even when dealing with the same situation.

This can be viewed as subjective, individual rationality, and as such it is recognized and dealt with in our models of decision-making. A problem arises, however, when individual subjectivity becomes group subjectivity; when everyone sees things in the same distorted or partial way (Ealau 1964; Janis 1972). While my interest is primarily with the effect of this type of behaviour upon the outcomes of individual organizations, it could also have the same type of effect upon an entire industrial sector, particularly one with a strong technological determinism. Halberstram's (1986) study of the American auto industry points out some of the consequences of this sort of industry-wide bias, as does Sampson's study of international banking (1981). It is possible that the failure of IBM to adapt to the changing computer environment; the spectacular failures in the savings and loan industry in the United States and the lesser degree of failure in the same industry in Canada; and the behaviour of banks in providing loans to the Third World in the 1970s and Olympia and York developments in the 1980s; can be explained by the existence of organizational bias. The decision-making process had become blinkered, producing a circumstance in which there was no one in management to suggest that the 'emperor has no clothes'.

In explaining budgetary decisions, then, the nature of the composition of the management groups may be an important factor. This aspect of management was recognized by the scientific management movement in the 1930s. Gulick (1937) discussed the problem that resulted as the 'professionalization' of management produced biases in perceptions of problems, and Fayol (1937) prescribed a management team which comes from widely diverse backgrounds. Yet the development of a limited perspective has since come to be viewed primarily as a positive feature of organizations, through the promotion of the development of 'corporate culture' or 'leadership vision' or management training. Corporate culture or philosophy is 'a relatively consistent, clearly formulated set of beliefs which specify the form of activities within the organization' (Hinings 1979: 140). It is expected and intended to contribute to the development of bias in outcomes, in the same way as any strongly held managerial value which constrains choice and inhibits recognition of error and adaptation (Jonsson and Lundin 1969; Sonnenfield 1981). Indeed, Bennis and Nanus (1985) have documented a number of cases in which an organizational bias, guided by an exceptional leader, was a positive force. The danger does not arise from bias *per se*, but from a situation in which the substance of a particular bias is incongruent with the problems facing an organization. The management, for example, is biased towards change when what may be needed is control. This type of circumstance can constitute a serious threat to the performance level of the organization and, ultimately, to its survival.

The advantage to considering the two forms of bias separately, rather than as one general category of 'culture', is that the factors that produce systemic bias are distinct from those that create managerial bias, and the effects of these two forms of bias are also largely independent. They are interconnected only to the extent that cultural values affect the type of managerial bias that exists, and its tendency to persist. In cultures where there is a strong desire for stability and a general respect for authority, a managerial bias, once created, would have a stronger tendency to persist. Changes to the management group would be less frequent as a result of the systemic bias. At the same time, cultural values can also affect the types of managerial bias which exist by producing a preference for particular types of management. Peters and Waterman (1982), in their discussion of American management, speculate that some common problems may arise from an American cultural preference for quantitative, hard solutions, and for managers who reflect this systemic bias. This is supported by studies of bureaucratic elites in the public sector, where generalists are less often found in the US senior bureaucracy than in those of other countries.

In time, organizations may adapt and correct for bias, but alternative values may often be too weak to overcome the original bias before outcomes have been seriously distorted over a long period, and they may be too weak to ever fully counterbalance a strong systemic bias. On a cross-cultural basis then, one would expect differing systemic biases to lead to variation in organizational outcomes in the long term. In the same way, the effects of managerial bias on the decision-making process are likely to be reflected in distortions in organizational outcomes. In some cases, these distortions may simply result in lower levels of performance than might be desirable. In other cases the results of unrecognized bias can be disastrous. Romzek and Dubnick (1987), for example, attribute the *Challenger* space shuttle catastrophe to an organizational bias in favour of the institutional and managerial goals of legitimation and control, rather than for technical concerns.

CONCLUSION

This chapter has identified two forms of bias or non-rational behaviour which are not incorporated within existing rational models of organizational behaviour. There are strong theoretical grounds for believing that these types of organizational bias can significantly affect the decisions and performance levels of organizations.

Systemic bias affects the values of all of the participants in the organization, including the management, and these values may limit the choices, search, and decision rules which are acceptable. It affects the information available to the organization; the definition of problems; and, more importantly, the consideration of alternatives and choice, with those alternatives which are inconsistent with cultural values being rejected or ignored. While a common culture makes it easier for an organization to operate by providing a common, known set of standards, it also limits the flexibility and adaptability of the organization.

The potential for managerial bias arises from the make up of the management of the organization. Managers' actions are constrained by their experience and knowledge of the organization, including their knowledge and experience of the organization's various sub-systems. As it is unlikely that they will have equal knowledge of all aspects of the organization, they will tend to favour those aspects of the organization that they know best. This is a broader instance of the standard organizational perception that the people around you are essential and hard-working, and it is the other guy who has (or is) slack. This can also take the form of general goal displacement when the goals of one sub-system or group within the organization become the goals of the organization. Thus, managerial bias will produce an organizational bias in cases in which the organization's management is dominated by membership from one sub-system of the organization, is able to replace itself, and remains in control over some period of time.

In the two chapters that follow the consequences of systemic and managerial bias are explored in more detail in the actions of the same organizations which were examined in Chapter 1. If it can be shown that these two sources of bias are important in explaining and predicting the discretionary budget decisions and the decision processes of organizations at this micro level, it is also reasonable to expect that they may have important consequences for the performance of these and other organizations over time.

3 The impact of managerial differences

INTRODUCTION

I am going to deal first with the question of managerial bias because it has the potential advantage that, while systemic factors are constants, management can perhaps be changed. Unlike the literature on culture and organizations, which is discussed in the next chapter, the literature on management rarely considers the effects on organizations of systematic variations in the knowledge and experience of those who run them. Instead, it deals with management as an undifferentiated group, or as subject only to demographic or random effects, or as a single individual (Pfeffer 1982; Hambrick and Mason 1984). But it may be that many of the paradoxes found within the research on management can be understood if the sub-system from which the members of the senior management group of the organization emanate is taken into consideration. In this chapter we consider the impact of bias resulting from specific management types on the outcomes of the organization. The logic of the argument tested in this chapter is twofold. The senior management of the organization which must, by definition, represent some combination of those sub-systems, will tend to be dominated by one sub-system of the organization; and managers from different sub-systems of the organization will tend to act differently.

The literature on organizations and management is not unconcerned with the characteristics of managers and their behaviour. We have all read biographies of successful managers who, eschewing conventional wisdom, came into a company, recognized its problems, and single-handedly turned it into an overnight success; or, alternatively, the post mortem exposés of those managers who could have avoided disaster but were not listened to. Leaving these supermen (or potential supermen) aside, the management decision-making literature is replete with questionnaire- or interview-based studies of how ordinary managers decide. Not surprisingly, this literature has found that they (and their organizations) carefully balance various factors in order to do the right thing. This, as I noted in Chapter 1, is the process which has been appropriately termed 'ex post hoc rationalization'.

What is less often done is to focus upon the management as a differentiated inner group in order to consider the impact upon the organization when this group varies systematically within industries and within countries.[1] Using the same companies as in Chapter 1, this chapter concentrates upon the effect that two different types of management configuration have upon resource allocations within these firms.

THE TYPES OF MANAGERS

It was clear from the discussion in Chapter 1 that there are differences among organizations in their outcome preferences and behaviour which remain unexplained by the neo-Weberian model. In the last chapter we considered how different biases could affect the pattern of decision-making and outcomes of organizations. In particular, I suggested that the composition of the management group can explain some differences between organizations.

The literature identifies the degree of entrepreneurial spirit, the type of tenure, and the method of succession of management as some of the relevant factors in determining managerial preferences, and it relates the values and preferences of management in times of change to factors such as the organization's age, environment, technology and size (Passmore 1988). But these factors may be related to a particular type of management, rather than acting as independent variables that affect preferences and responses to the contingency factors.

Managerial bias develops when one sub-system of the organization comes to dominate the goal setting and decision processes of the organization such that the knowledge and experience of management relates primarily to one aspect of the firm's activities. For example, when an accountant explains that poor cash-flow management was the reason that four different real estate companies for which he worked went broke, the question that arises (in addition, to the obvious one of the individual's professional competence) is whether that was the cause, or merely the cause he is best able to identify.[2]

The source of bias is a set of values or knowledge shared by most of the members of the management group that precludes their seeing the whole of the organization and incorporating new knowledge. It can be either an unacknowledged variable or an explicit factor, such as a corporate philosophy which is stated and used as one of the decision-rules in making choices.

The recognition of biased cognitive perceptions on the part of managers is certainly not new. It is a phenomenon long known to psychologists and easily substantiated by anyone reading the business pages of their local newspaper. Thus, when the managers of bankrupt firms blame changes in the environment for their failure, we are not surprised (Sutton and Callahan 1988). But we may wonder why other firms in the same environment did not similarly fail. This tendency to see the cause of a problem as some group other than yours, and the solution to be action on the part of someone other than you, is not uncommon (Kaufman 1985). It can, however, become particularly important to organizations when one component or sub-system within the organization dominates the decision-making process.

Given the three sub-systems identified in Chapter 1, there are seven possible types of management configuration. Three are cases of domination by only one sub-system, three are domination by two of the three sub-systems, and one includes representation from all three sub-systems. Even in firms with a strong preference for hiring only one type of manager, it is unlikely that cases in which only one sub-system was represented would be typical. For example, legal requirements for corporate controllers or corporate secretaries who are accountants or lawyers would tend to ensure some managerial representation in all companies. But, as I discussed in the last chapter, sub-system domination is likely to occur in most organizations, and even across many industries.

When categorizing management as being from one of three sub-systems, one of which is the managerial sub-system, there is inevitably some confusion in the terms. There are managers or management defined as being part of the managerial sub-system, and there is the senior management or upper echelon of the organization made up of representatives from some combination of the three sub-systems. In the literature on public organizations the term administrator and administration is traditionally used in place of manager or management. For purposes of clarity, therefore, I will follow that convention by referring to the administrative sub-system. Dominance by that sub-system will be considered as administrative management, or management which may demonstrate an administrative bias.

The definition of the three sub-systems is not altogether unproblematic. In the first place, it is recognized that lawyers and accountants do not act alike. While they would both be expected to be concerned with control within the organization, they are likely to prefer different instruments of control – although the emphasis remains on control rather than production. In the second place, both the corporate controller and the corporate secretary, while concerned with control, could also be considered to be part of the institutional rather than the administrative sub-system, their role being to ensure that external institutional standards are being met. I return to this question in Chapter 6 when a broader range of firms is considered. This did not become a problem within the three specific industries studied here.

While institutional components could be identified within the organizations in this portion of the study, only within the banks did they represent a clear subset of functions (and one rarely represented within the management group). As the senior public affairs executive in one bank pointed out, he would never reach the upper echelons of management as he was not perceived within the organization as a 'real' banker, despite having been with the bank for all of his career. Within this set of companies the institutional component generally tended to overlap with aspects of the administrative or technical sub-system.

The more common distinction between the technical and administrative sub-system, however, is relatively straightforward and has more intuitive meaning. At this point I am not interested in demonstrating that one form of manager or management type is necessarily better, but rather that they are in important ways different – although firms with technical management on average did have higher profit levels. An extreme case points out the differences in the two management types. A senior executive in a construction company who expresses both a lack of interest in, and lack of knowledge of, the housing market, but who has an avid interest in, and keen knowledge of, financial control systems and computerized personnel systems, clearly represents the administrative sub-system. Another construction executive, on the other hand, whose primary interest lies in seeing every project and every house built by the company – and discussing construction techniques with the site superintendents – is an obvious representative of the technical sub-system.

These individual characteristics become a problem when most of the members of the senior management of the organization exhibit the same concerns. The two cases above would only be illustrative of organizational bias if all of the senior management spent their time dealing with computerized control systems and never visited a construction site; or, alternatively, spent a high proportion of their time on site visits talking to the construction superintendents while showing no concern with ensuring that invoices went out.

The characteristic behaviour of the management types is at least partially predictable. Hofstede, for example, found that people 'in accounting, planning and control roles tend to stress the form of activities, while people in operating roles tend to stress content' (1980: 158). An organization in which the administrative sub-system is most powerful, one utilizing primarily a managerial technology, is likely to consider a problem as one of control, and to institute search procedures within its own sub-system. Accordingly, it will concern itself with internal measures of performance, and legal procedures, and will emphasize 'control and rationality by numbers' (Mintzberg 1983: 492). It would also be expected to be less concerned with industry norms as its managers might be unfamiliar with such standards.

In cases where the technical sub-system is most powerful, the organization would have a bias towards concern with the product and the production process, and would be expected to favour production solutions. It would be able to recognize problems arising from broader market or economic trends, but would tend to ignore problems of organizational control and co-ordination.

The key to effectiveness in terms of sub-system representation and behaviour, however, is not the question of how these various types of managerial configurations might behave but the assumption that the sub-system (or sub-systems) in control of the organization are those which are best suited to the needs of the organization. I return to this point in Chapter 6. My initial concern is with organizations which exhibit managerial bias in one of two forms – technical or administrative sub-system dominance within their senior management. These would be expected to be the most common forms of organizational dominance: technical, because the organization was formed to do something, and in all likelihood by someone who knew how to do it; and administrative, because the co-ordinative aspects of the administrative sub-system have come to be synonymous with our understanding of the role of management – the familiar PODSCORB functions of planning, organizing, directing, staffing, co-ordinating, reporting and budgeting.

The role of management in the construction and finance sector

There are few studies that relate managerial characteristics and behaviour to administrative components in the financial and residential development industries. Those studies which do exist recognize that differences in management may be a relevant factor in determining organizational outcomes, but are unclear about what aspects of management or management type are most important.

Among the studies of the banking industry and banking performance, only McClelland (1981) specifically considered management type. His study of two banks found a relationship between strategy and structure, on the one hand, and management, and level of performance, on the other. His Sherman Bank, an example of administrative management drawn primarily from outside the industry, developed a large strategic corporate head office staff, and moved away from banking as it diversified. In this study, Bankers Trust followed a similar pattern, bringing in a number of outside senior managers in the late 1970s, emphasizing 'improving decision-making through analytical tools,' and, in 1983, virtually withdrew from traditional banking activities. McClelland's General Bank of Chicago is an example of technical management run entirely by long-time bankers. It did not have a large corporate staff and diversified into traditional banking areas. In my sample, both Manufacturer's Hanover and the Royal Bank of Canada are similar to the General Bank of Chicago. Both are referred to as 'banker's banks', with senior executives having long-term service with their company, and in most cases having joined the bank directly out of university.[3]

Other studies have found more contradictory evidence. In studying the level of administrative costs and performance, it was found that size was not a factor in Chicago banks (Coates and Updegaff 1973), but it was in Israeli banks (Mannheim and Moscovitz 1979). Similarly, there is confusion about the impact of ownership. In one case it was found that owners of banks took fewer risks (Jessee and Seelig 1977), a finding which was not replicated by later studies (Kold 1981; Kwast and Rose 1982). The conclusion reached by Tainio *et al.* (1991) in studying Finnish banks may serve as a summary: 'explanations of bank performance are more dynamic and context dependent' than previously found.

There is, however, flowing through this literature an implicit, if not explicit, recognition that it is something to do with the management which may be the determining characteristic. Mannheim and Moscovitz found that larger firms have lower administrative costs because of their preference for control by rules. Graham *et al.* found that in Canada it was not possible to draw conclusions about institutional conventions accepted 'by all companies combined, since what one company will not do, another may do' (1962: 37). Lermer (1978) suggests that it is the attitude of management towards risk-taking that is relevant, with lower risk firms having lower administrative costs and lower average profits. Atkinson suggests that it is differences in management priorities and responses to the environment which are important in distinguishing among firms in the US savings and loan industry, rather than differences in ownership. 'The form of ownership also appears to be of more theoretical than real world significance in its effect on the freedom of the management of the firm' (Atkinson 1974: 4).

It is possible that the serious problems faced by the savings and loans industry in the United States, and the less serious problems faced by the same industry in Canada, during the late 1980s resulted in part from a change in the environment as a consequence of deregulation, but also from change in the type of management and managerial bias which existed within the industry. Instead of the strongly held 'fiduciary' value which had dominated the technical managers for decades, a new widely held value that involved paying only lip service to the letter of regulatory requirements took hold, in part because many of the senior managers were not experienced in the industry. A senior loan company official with more than forty years' experience in the industry painstakingly distinguished between types of loans companies and their operations. There were 'managers who crunch numbers, lenders who understand their purpose is to match terms, and entrepreneurs interested only in a fast profit and who will lend on anything'. This may have been the behaviour behind Lermer's observation:

> Two firms with the same number of depositors, loans and other activities, may nevertheless be producing quite different total outputs if one firm's strategy is to match the term of maturity of its assets and liabilities, whereas the other lends longer in term than it borrows. The former firm will require fewer resources in managing its asset liability portfolio and will, in the long run, earn lower average profits than the second.
>
> (Lermer 1978: 5)

The literature on 'merchant builders' is even less conclusive. Generally a considerable amount of time is spent on the background, personalities and experience of the management of the companies without trying to find any pattern in their behaviour (Lorimer 1976; Goldenberg 1981). Grebler (1973) considered the personality of the founder more important than his background, training and experience, but went on to state that those trained in business administration adapt more easily. His recipe for success is a balanced management type – 'an admixture of industry expertise and general management talent' (Grebler 1973: 69). Studies of financial institutions and the residential development industry, then, while rarely focusing upon management, suggest that there are unexplained variations between organizations. It may be that different types of senior management can explain these differences.

IDENTIFYING MANAGEMENT TYPES

For the purpose of this study it is assumed that organizations are run by their senior management. It is their preferences which the organization will reflect, albeit imperfectly. There may be small groups within the organization which at times have inordinate power, but their power will either emanate from, or be reflected in, the fact that a representative of their group is included within the senior management group. Staff positions frequently carry more power than their formal position within the organization would indicate. The literature on succession and simple logic, however, both suggest that the preferences and biases of these individuals will usually reflect the preferences and biases of the manager to whom they are responsible. It is not being suggested that managers are either so narrow or so inept that they are incapable of considering factors other than those central to their own experience, but rather that there will be a predisposition to define problems and consider solutions related to this experience. Management is defined as the five senior operating executives within the organization. This usually consisted of the top two management levels within the organization. When it was not clear from the organizational chart who the top five executives were, or in cases in which a number of senior executives had the same title, the five most highly paid managers were included. Management type was determined by considering the background and experience of the majority of members of that group. A technical manager was defined as one who had spent at least half of his career within the same industry and whose educational background and experience within the industry was in an area related to the technical or production aspects. An administrative manager was defined as someone whose educational background was in an area related to managerial aspects of the organization and whose work experience was either outside the industry or entirely within the administrative sub-system.

The typical career pattern for technical bankers was to join the bank as a teller and move up, for technical developers it was to found the firm. Administrative managers in both industries were usually hired for some specialized expertise at a mid-level in the organization and rose to the top. Often they changed the overall management type as they took control. In the loan industry the pattern was not as clear. Some technical managers followed a typical 'banker' career, while others started (or were part of the long-time senior management of) the company and developed their expertise over time and at the top. Administrative managers tended to follow the same pattern as in the other industries, but there was also a tendency for them to be newcomers to the industry who were hired at the top or who bought the firm. Administrative managers most commonly had an educational background in law or general business, although in the development companies finance was also common. There was one example, not part of this sample, of a developer buying a loan company for his son as a graduation present when he completed his MBA at Harvard. (I should point out that the firm has been quite successful.)

Some cases were not entirely clear. For example, a lawyer joined a trust company as his first job, held a number of positions within both the technical and administrative sub-systems of the company, and eventually rose to be the executive vice-president of customer services. What type of manager is he? In this case, the decision was made that, despite the breadth of his experience and his education, he had spent more of his time within the technical than the administrative sub-system and he was classified as a technical manager. Generally, in cases in which training and experience were from different sub-systems, experience was used as the basis of classification. Another example is a lawyer who spent most of his working life in the technical sub-system (land development and construction) of a development company. He developed considerable experience, and it is assumed knowledge, of development techniques. He was classified as a technical manager. In practice, these types of problems arose infrequently. The consistency of career paths was quite striking and crossovers between sub-systems were relatively rare. Those without technical knowledge tended not to become involved in the technical sub-system and those with administrative training tended not to spend long periods of time in the industry.[4]

The management of each organization was classified as either administrative or technical in each year of the study. Technical management includes those cases in which four or more of the five senior executives had spent most of their working lives within the technical sub-system of the firm or industry. Administrative management includes those cases in which four of the five executives had spend most of their working lives in staff or support functions, or in management positions outside of the industry.

Cases in which less than four of the five executives represented the same sub-system were to have been classified as balanced management which did not exhibit any discernible bias. This would be the case that Grebler suggested was the ideal. Surprisingly, only four cases were found. Two firms had a balanced management for two years each while they were undergoing a transition from one management type to the other. Consistently, firms had an almost overwhelming representation from one sub-system or the other. When changes in management took place, it tended to represent a larger change-over in the management group over a one- or two-year period.

For the early years of this study the Canadian development company, Cadillac-Fairview, provides a good example of technical management. Four of the five senior managers were trained as engineers or architects and had spent their entire working lives in the construction industry. Similarly, many of the banks had management groups in which all had started as tellers or junior staff in a branch office. On the other hand, a good example of administrative management is found again in Cadillac-Fairview in the latter period of the study. No one in the senior management group had either a background or experience in the construction industry. It should be noted that shortly after the shift in management type the organization also left the construction industry.[5]

When management type is added to our model from Chapter 1 the explanatory ability of the model improves considerably. For the level of administrative costs (ACR), it goes from 31 per cent to 38 per cent. A more dramatic improvement is seen in the changes to the ACR level (or the rate of adaptation) where the model's explanatory power increases to 29 per cent from only 8 per cent.[6] It is of limited interest, however, simply to know that adding a variable 'improves the model'. We want to understand how

Table 3.1 Variables by type of management 1971–82 (mean levels)

	Administrative management	Technical management
Administrative Cost Ratio (ACR)* (%)	16	19
Annual change in ACR* (%)	0.16	0.41
Size (assets in millions)[a]	14,910	12,880
Environment (% annual change in revenues)	23	23
Performance (% annual return on revenue)*	5	7
Total number	135	224

Notes: * Significant at the 0.05 level.
[a] The size of the organizations is indicated by assets measured in the currency of the country in which they are located.

knowing the management type of the organization can improve our ability to comprehend the decisions made about administrative costs and, in particular, the tendency of the organization to adapt by making changes in its administrative cost level.

As was discussed in Chapter 1, it is generally accepted that organizations follow standard operating rules or rules of thumb. But the standard operating rules (SOR) followed by organizations may vary systematically as a result of the type of management configuration, and the nature of sub-system dominance within the organization.

Table 3.1 provides the mean levels for the variables by management type. Despite operating in an environment which is similar and being of similar size, the two types of management do have differences in their average levels of the administrative cost ratio and a small difference in the level of change in the ACR.

The key finding is that administrative managers tend to have lower – and slightly more stable – administrative cost ratios. Why? One possibility is that because they have a preference for control, administrative managers are more aware of and more concerned with levels of administrative costs – which we must remember are discretionary costs. It could also be that larger firms are more likely to be able to capture economies of scale – and also more likely to be managed by administrative managers. To the extent that they have a bias towards this sub-system, they might also have a greater reluctance to adapt by reducing the level of administrative costs – or have more entrenched administrative cost levels. Technical management, on the other hand, may be more prepared to act to protect the technical core of the organization and, therefore, would be more prepared to change administrative cost levels. As one technical developer put it, 'when things start to

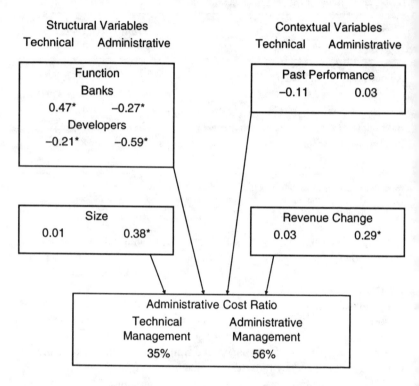

Figure 3.1 The impact of managerial bias on budget decisions

Note: *t-statistic significant at 0.05 level.

slip, I look around for someone I don't need and fire them'. Technical managers relative lack of concern with co-ordination and control could also explain their higher administrative cost levels.

But despite their lower administrative costs, administrative managers do not translate what could be considered higher levels of efficiency into greater profits. The average profit margin for technical managers is notably higher than that for administrative managers.

Figure 3.1 gives the relative strength of the model for determining the ACR for both management types. The figures for technical managers appear to the left of the variable name, figures for administrative managers are on the right. As in Chapter 1, the figures within the boxes are the standardized regression coefficients which give the relative importance of the variable. The numbers at the bottom give the percentage of the variation which is explained. If all managers acted alike, or if all managers acted differently in an unsystematic way, the two sets of numbers would be about the same. This is not the case. They are quite different, indicating that there is a systematic impact of management type as I have defined it. Now let us consider the extent to which these differences are consistent with how we would expect the two different management types, or types of managers, to act.

The first thing to note is that the model is considerably more effective in predicting the behaviour of administrative managers. It can explain 56 per cent of the variation in their actions compared with only 35 per cent in the case of technical managers. Technical managers behave in more idiosyncratic ways, while administrative managers tend to conform more closely to the expectations of the rational model. This may simply reflect the fact that the training of administrative managers often includes teaching 'appropriate' responses to factors such as function, size, and environmental change as it is reflected in revenues.

Contextual variables have no impact for technical managers while revenue change is important for administrative managers. The structural variable of function is important for both types of managers but size is not relevant for the technical managers. The general relationship of increasing size producing economies of scale does not hold, nor does the related explanation that it is because administrative managers are in larger organizations that they capture economies of scale. The larger the size of the administratively managed firm, the higher the level of ACR.

Certainly, we would expect technical managers to be more sensitive to the 'rules of thumb' or SORs of their industry. This is clear when we look at the relationship between the function groups. For technical managers banks have ACR levels above those of loan companies, reflecting no doubt the greater complexity of their operations. Similarly, development companies, which are the least complex of the three types of industry, have the lowest levels of ACR. For administrative managers the pattern is different. Loan companies have the highest level of administrative costs (i.e. the relationship is negative for both the other functional groups). It is possible that the loan companies had the weakest SORs, thus making it easier for 'high-flier' administrative managers to move resources to their own subsystem. This may explain some of the problems the industry faced later in the 1980s.

With respect to adaptation, the model is better at predicting changes in the administrative cost ratios for technical managers. For both management types change in administrative costs are related only to changes in the contextual variables, with changes in revenue being the most important. When things are good, they increase their spending on overhead and discretionary costs and when revenues decline, they cut them. For technical

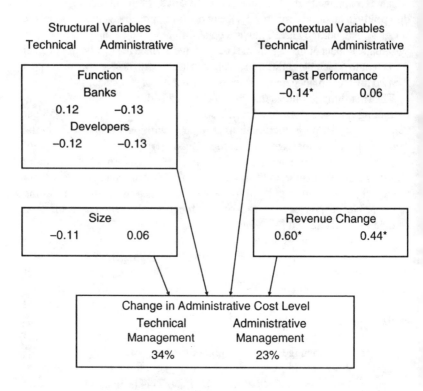

Figure 3.2 The impact of managerial bias on adaptation

Note: *t-statistic significant at 0.05 level.

managers, there is also a notable negative relationship with past performance, albeit only one-quarter as strong as the relationship with the environment. When profits decline they are more likely to increase their administrative costs, perhaps it takes poor performance to stimulate their interest in better control. An alternative explanation is that when profits decline, they place their emphasis upon improving productive efficiency by lowering production costs. The nature of the ratio is such that lowering production costs while administrative costs remain stable raises the level of the ACR.

Overall, technical managers are more responsive to changes in revenue and performance than administrative managers. Administrative managers tend to hold the relationship between production and administrative costs more stable – irrespective of performance. This may reflect an unwillingness to sacrifice administrative costs even when profits decline.

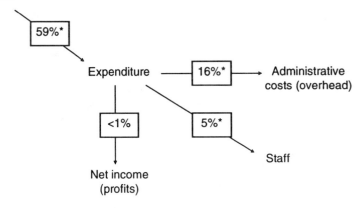

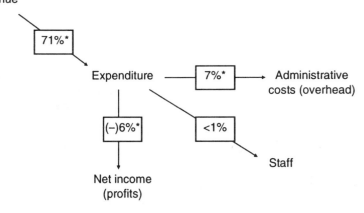

Figure 3.3 Paths of decision-making

Notes: Statistics are r-square values showing the percentage of the variation in the rates of
change of pairs of variables which can be statistically explained.
*t-statistic significant at 0.05 level.

There does, therefore, appear to be systematic differences in the way the
two management types react.

Figure 3.3 provides an indication of the differences in decision patterns
and preferences of the two management types. In Chapter 1 we looked at
the decision path which showed how various costs moved together. When

we consider the same path for the two management types separately, the pattern changes dramatically and makes more intuitive sense. For administrative managers changes in revenue account for 71 per cent of changes in expenditures; for technical managers only 59 per cent.[7] Administrative managers have only a slight tendency, however, to change administrative costs, and none to change staff (the actual figure is 0.0001 per cent). As expected, administrative managers appear to consider staff as more strongly entrenched, in that changes in staff do not correlate with changes in revenue, expenditures or administrative costs. For technical managers the levels are higher, corroborating the comment of the developer cited earlier. While less likely to adjust expenditures to match revenues, when they do so, technical managers are more willing to adjust both administrative costs and staff. When we consider the relationship with after tax profits, there is also a difference by management type. While technical managers show no relationship between expenditures and income, among administrative managers there is a negative relationship. This may indicate that administrative managers are more cautious, placing a greater emphasis on stability in their unwillingness to alter fixed costs.[8]

Administrative managers are more inclined to adjust expenditures to match changes in revenue, but the correlation between overall expenditures and administrative costs is lower than for technical managers. This reflects a bias towards protecting the administrative component at the expense of the production component. There is no correlation between changes in staff and any of the other variables under administrative management, which supports a conclusion of a bias against changing fixed costs. Technical managers, on the other hand, are less responsive to changes in revenue, but the relationships indicate a greater willingness to change overhead and staff.

It is often assumed that in some industries differences in management are a result of differences in behaviour between owner-managers and hired managers.[9] But these differences in behaviour may result not from ownership *per se*, but rather from a tendency for hired managers to be more likely to be trained in managerial activities, while owners may be more likely to be familiar with the technical sub-system. For example, our finding that technical managers are more sensitive to performance could be because they were owners. The firms studied included a mixture of both types of ownership. The banks within the study are exclusively run by hired managers; the loan companies are split with some owners and some hired managers in each country; and the developers are mainly owner-managed. There is, however, almost no relationship between management type and ownership (r^2=2 per cent). The apparent consequences of management types do not, therefore, actually reflect differences in the form of ownership.

Zimmerman (1991) found that stability of management was also related to organizational performance, with stability of management being a key factor in successful turnarounds. Thus, there is the possibility that relationships between management type and organizational outcomes might result in fact from differences in the frequency of management change. The average number of management changes per company for the two management types was actually identical at 9.7 each. There was a slightly higher level of management change among the widely held firms with the mean number of changes being 11.2 over the eleven years versus 9.5 for the owner controlled firms.[10]

It does seem, then, that differences in management type do produce differences in the importance that the variables in the model have in altering administrative costs. The expectation of sub-system dominance and managerial bias is relatively well supported.

THE IMPACT OF MANAGEMENT

This chapter has introduced the notion of managerial bias into the model and the analysis has shown that if we know the type of management we are better able to predict not only the level of administrative costs, but the rate of change of these costs. More importantly, we have also shown that the degree to which organizations respond to internal or external factors varies systematically not only by function and size, but also by management type. The findings indicate that administrative managers are reluctant to change administrative costs and tend to prefer income smoothing and a more entrenched administrative structure. Similarly, administrative managers are more responsive to the environment but do so by emphasizing control (and increased levels of administrative spending) in times of environment downturn. On the other hand, technical managers are more sensitive to the norms of their industry than to any other factor. Firms with technical management are inclined to have higher administrative costs but they are more prepared to adjust them to match changes in revenues or performance which may explain their higher overall profit levels.

The fact that management type does affect organizational decision-making and outcomes can help us to explain three interesting contradictions found in the literature on managerial and firm behaviour. The first relates to the relationship between ownership and performance; the second to the impact of changes in management upon organizational performance; and the third to the causes of high levels of administrative intensity.

As organizations become larger, they are more likely to be run by 'hired' managers, those whose 'best interests' lie in the direction of organizational survival (Weinshall 1977). These managerially controlled firms exercise income-smoothing to a greater extent than owner-controlled firms. Thus, they are more inclined to try to achieve consistent, but sub-optimal results (Baldwin 1964). This form of behaviour is consistent with theories of self-interest maximizing and bureaucratic growth (Williamson 1963; Niskanen 1971; Downs 1967). Thus the relationship between size, owner-ship and profits may be explained by the factor which has been introduced in this chapter – management type.

A similar contradiction is found in the literature on management change and performance. While changing managers is a common prescription for improving performance, it is not entirely clear that it is effective. Brown (1982), in a study of National Football League coaches, found that changing managers made little difference; while Pfeffer and Davis-Blake (1986), in a study of National Basketball Association coaches, found the exact opposite. Similarly, Starbuck *et al.* (1978), in studies of European manufacturing firms, found that it was necessary to bring in new management in order to achieve change; but Hall's (1976) study of the decline of the *Saturday Evening Post* seems to indicate that a change in management accelerated the decline.

What these studies fail to consider is the background and experiences of the management group rather than simply the most senior manager. Second, they do not consider the possibility that differences in education and experience could produce systematic differences between managers, or differences in management type, which would lead one type of manager to be successful and another to be unsuccessful. Thus, they tend to assume that all 'hired' managers will act alike, but at the same time assume that 'new' management will behave differently. These contradictory findings may result from these false assumptions. They may be explained by examining, as I have, not different managers but different types of managers and the biases of different types of management. We found, for example, that technical managers on average had higher levels of performance. Zimmer-man's study of the turnaround of sixteen firms whose survival was threatened provides support for this thesis. Looking at firms from 1900 through to 1988, the key to a successful turnaround was that management at the 'successful firms had extensive experience in the particular industry or a closely related industry' (1991: 259).

The literature on public policy provides a number of examples of differences in policy outcomes attributable to differences in the training and experience of the senior policy makers which is discussed in greater detail in Chapter 6. Indeed, the assumption that the training and experience of civil servants biases outcomes is central to the literature of public adminis-tration and public policy (Derlien 1992).

Other studies of firms in crises where management change took place support our finding that it may not be the change *per se* which is important, but a change in the type of management. In those cases in which the bias was overcome and the organization survived, it was as a result of changes in the sub-systems represented in the management group. A Business International study (1987) of 'restructuring and turnaround' in twenty-seven firms found that changing management, or using a management consultant with a different perspective, was the most common recipe for a successful turnaround during the 1980s. Earlier studies of mismanagement and failure during the 1970s also found that inflexibility was the common problem, and that adaptation took place only when the passive groups found that action was necessary to rescue their own interests and the organization itself (Dunbar and Goldberg 1978). Often this took the form of bankers or a major stockholder forcing restructuring upon the organization. Recovery was usually associated with a change in management ideology which accompanied the change in the management itself, a change which produced a new perspective which was unbiased (or at least had a different bias).

Yet, Hall's (1976) study of the *Saturday Evening Post* can be seen as a case where the new management of the organization was dominated by accountants and controllers who did not understand the technical sub-system of the organization – in this case magazine publishing – and who were biased towards defining problems and choosing alternatives which dealt with the managerial aspects of the organization. The dominance of the managerial component was also found to be a cause of failure by Zimmerman (1991), who found in addition that stability of management was more common in the case of successful turnarounds. As we have seen in this chapter, it was neither ownership, nor management change which made a difference, but management type.

Finally, we turn to the question of administrative costs. It has been commonplace to assume that administrative costs increase with time and size, but that very large organizations also experience some economies of scale. But Freeman and Hannan (1975) found that organizations that had experienced unusually rapid increases in their administrative components during times of growth also tended to be slow to reduce administrative costs when they entered a period of tight resources. The administrative costs were protected. Studies of hospitals, however, indicate that this is not always the case (Kriesberg 1962; Meyer 1985). The nature of the composition of the management group also needs to be taken into consideration. Freeman and Hannan's (1975) findings can be explained by virtue of the budget decisions within school boards being made by administrators who place a high level of importance upon administrative activities.

It would follow, then, that many of the findings related to the administrative components of organizations may be based on a common type of organization, one in which the administrative sub-system dominates decision-making. For example, as organizations become more specialized and differentiated they tend to place more emphasis upon administrative or control activities (Mintzberg 1983: Ch. 2). But if older, larger and more specialized firms are more likely to be managed by representatives of the administrative sub-system, it is the preferences and knowledge of that group that leads to the increase in the size of the administrative component of the organization. At the same time owner-managers, particularly if they founded the firm, are more likely to represent the technical sub-system.

CONCLUSION

This chapter has provided support for the contention that different management types produce different outcomes despite similarities in size, function, and the environment – presumably as a result of systematic differences in preferences between the two types of management configurations. Thus organizational bias does develop from differences in management type.

These findings also tend to understate the variations which exist between firms. We have assumed that all managers from one sub-system will act alike. This is obviously a simplification, a fact which is emphasized by the following two quotations about the philosophy of two technically managed banks. 'We believe it is our obligation to assume a reasonable degree of risk in our lending activities. It would have been unfortunate if the banks had moved precipitously to recoup on loans by forcing the troubled borrower to liquidate assets in a distressed market or forced them into bankruptcy.' That sentence contrasts with, '[t]he word forgiveness is loaded with seductively attractive emotional baggage, and it should surprise no one that it finds such favour with observers who are not commercial bankers. . . . Forgiveness does take place in commercial banking – but it marks the end, not the beginning, of a relationship. . . . For us, forgiveness is logically, pragmatically and commercially unacceptable.'[11]

The relevance of bias for the long-term survival of the firm may be greatest during periods in which the environment is unfavourable. Jonsson and Lundin (1971) make the point that although management is affected by 'waves of myths' which influence decision-making, these myths break down in times of crisis. These two findings both are consistent with our expectation of bias. Myths, when they arise, are followed regardless of their objective applicability in the belief that they will be successful. Thus, the myth of 'mean and lean' will be followed even if it is not the appropriate response for that firm in that circumstance. This constitutes an example of the dominant administrative sub-system's bias with no countervailing influence from the technical sub-system. Such an overemphasis upon the administrative sub-system and its values is a characteristic that some writers such as Robert Reich (1983) and others (Kilman 1989; Pasmore 1988; Zimmerman 1991) have argued is a major source of the lack of competitiveness of North American industry.

This draws our attention to systemic bias and the influence of systemic values – those values which are unlikely to change, but which must be taken into consideration if managerial bias is to be dealt with. In the next chapter we turn to this problem.

4   Systemic differences
The role of culture

INTRODUCTION

In a world in which 'globalization' is viewed as the predominant business trend, the extent to which the people within organizations, and the organizations themselves, are 'culture-bound' is of increasing importance. 'Culture-bound' in this sense means the extent to which deeply held systemic values affect the decision-making process within the organization.

Systemic values can affect an organization in three ways – through the values of the participants in the organization; through a preference for managers whose values and management style are consistent with the cultural bias; and through the structure. It follows that these values will have a direct effect on decisions by altering the outcome preferences of the majority of the members, and the knowledge which they utilize; and an indirect effect upon outcomes by way of the intervening variables, structure and the values of the individual participants. On a cross-cultural basis, then, one would expect differing systemic biases to lead to variation in organizational outcomes in the long term, but management studies of organizations in different countries or cultures tend to emphasize variations in structure or management attitudes rather than differences in the decision-making process within the organizations themselves (Child and Tayeb 1982–3; Everett *et al.* 1982; Hofstede 1980; Jenner 1982).

This chapter adds cultural or systemic bias to our model of organizational decision-making. The results suggest that the relative importance of the structural and contextual factors vary depending upon the systemic bias that results from the cultural values of the society in which the organization operates. Moreover, not only do the factors which are important in decision-making vary considerably from one cultural context to another, but the impact of managerial bias also varies across countries.

THE CULTURE-BOUND ORGANIZATION

Cultural or systemic values closely meet our conditions for organizational bias because they represent situations in which the values and beliefs held by all or most of the participants in an organization constrain the actions of the organization in making decisions consistent with the exigencies of the task environment.

Within the 'comparative administration' or 'culture and management' literature, historically there have been two trains of thought about the role of culture. One, the 'convergence thesis' originally associated with the work of Harbison and Myers (1959), argues that differences in structure and management practices are the result of a lack of technological development. 'There is a general logic of management development which has applicability to advanced and industrializing countries in the modern world' (Harbison and Myers 1959: 177). According to this viewpoint, cultural differences reflect an evolutionary process of management style, moving through the patrimonial, to the political and finally to the professional – with professional being the ideal. The main problem with this approach is that because it is primarily American-based, it tended to treat American values and the needs of technological development as synonymous (Jamieson 1982–3; Mouzelis 1968: 175). Thus, it did not recognize that, even with professional forms of management, there can be wide variations in the form of professionalism across cultures.

This approach, while remaining the dominant perspective in the United States (Adler, 1983a; Czarniawska-Joerges, 1992), lost ground in the European literature during the 1970s. It has, however, experienced a resurgence in research on international management which focuses upon transnational firms. As much of this research is based on questionnaires and interviews, it tends to reflect what managers say, think or believe that they or their companies do (Business International 1987; Everett *et al.* 1982). To the extent that the research is done by American academics or management consultants, the questions asked may also reflect the cultural bias of the researcher. If we are going to transplant management practices, and managers, across cultures, it is important to understand the extent to which factors in the decision-process vary from one country to another in a more objective fashion.

The second approach, while recognizing that technological progress and economic growth will affect organizations, maintains that culture does make a difference (Child and Tayeb 1982). Its main argument is that different cultures produce differences in structure and managerial behaviour independent of other conditions. These studies of the effect of cultural distinctions tend to fall into three groups:

1   studies of management behaviour or technique;
2   studies of the effect of culture on structure; and
3   studies of bureaucracies and the bureaucratic process.

The distinction between the first two is illustrated by the classic case of Theory Z (Ouchi 1981). It was originally embraced as a 'new' approach to management which would allow Western countries in general, and the United States in particular, to emulate the economic success of Japan, an example of the first type of study. From attempts to introduce the technique in the United States it soon became apparent that it overlooked cultural traits in Japan which made such a management style possible. Japanese success was due to these traits as much as to the management style itself, and the transplanting of the technique was neither possible, nor would it be effective, without considerable adaptation to the culture into which it was to be translated (Baar and Tomako 1988; Jaeger 1982–3). In effect, it was a better example of the second type of study in showing the relationship between culture and management than simply a study of management technique.

Studies of managerial behaviour are primarily concerned with the styles of management which are most acceptable to various cultural groups. Findings indicate that both employee expectations and styles of management in such areas as incentive systems, control systems and promotion patterns vary systematically across cultures on a continuum from authoritarian to participatory. Some of these studies consider only one organization, but one operating in a number of countries (Clark 1985; Conference Board 1973). The author's aim is usually to reduce the effect of national cultures on the behaviour of multinationals, and to improve their performance, by suggesting ways of fostering a strong organizational culture. The emphasis tends to be upon management techniques, and methods of balancing the needs for decentralization and communication with regional operations with that of maintaining control. Consider, for example, the recommendations from the BIR study of management turnarounds:

> Local operations in most firms are traditionally managed by individuals whose allegiance is split between the company and local interests. Therefore, when a company decentralizes internationally, it may be in the firm's interest to appoint expatriates to manage certain local units in order to retain sufficient control.

> (Business International 1987: 38)

A second, well-established consequence of systemic bias is found in the structural characteristics of organizations. Studies carried out in the late 1960s and 1970s tended to view the influence of culture as yet another contingency variable, together with technology and task environment, that differentiates the structures of organizations. Most of these studies deal with organizations of a particular type, such as manufacturing firms or financial institutions, in two or three countries. Generally, the tendency has been to emphasize the supra-national similarities of structural charac- teristics rather than cross-national differences in behaviour. But there have also been significant findings of cross-national differences. This relation- ship between structure and culture has been studied and summarized extensively, to yield an impressive body of empirical information.[1] We know, for example, that the relationships among size, the centralization of decision-making and the degree of hierarchy, vary across cultural groups. What is not as clear is the relationship between structure and performance.

The political science literature has been far more aware of the impact of systemic factors on organizations. Early studies of administrative elites highlighted the effect of differences in training and conditions of entry on public administration. Building on the early work of Weber (1966) and Finer (1941), their findings support the Weberian notion of a trend towards bureaucratization in societies, but demonstrate that the forms of control and, more particularly, the actions of individuals within the organization, vary with cultural patterns (Armstrong 1973; Crozier 1964). While these studies focused primarily upon elites, another set of studies carried out by political scientists has looked at the relationship between institutions and organizational outcomes and performance. Studies of political outcomes tended to emphasize differences in the decision-making processes within countries and the education of bureaucratic elites (Putman *et al.* 1988; Suleiman 1984), and have only recently begun to consider structures and institutions and the broader effects these have upon overall economic performance.[2]

Thus, the training and succession patterns of elites within the bureau- cracy and the structure of the bureaucracy influence the policy-making process (Carroll 1990c). At the same time, these patterns and structures vary across cultures (Aberbach *et al.* 1981). The effect is to influence institutional constraints such as styles of regulation and forms of interven- tion (Vogel 1986). Finally, the institutions of politics and administration have been found to affect systematically the forms of intervention in the economy, and the response and performance of industries (Cawson *et al.* 1990; Coleman 1988; Zysman 1983). These studies have shown, then, that national identity continues to matter.

This relationship between culture, political systems and institutions has been a matter of debate in the political science literature for decades (Almond and Verba 1965; Atkinson and Coleman 1985). Although political theory has recognized the problems inherent in distinguishing the direction of the causal link between these factors, management theory has tended to view culture, and a bewildering number of definitions of the term, as the preceding variable (Khandwalla 1977; Neghandi 1983). The term systemic, therefore, is used in a manner that is common in political science and sociology to refer to the interrelationship between the cultural values and the political and social institutions of a country. For example, in the United States traditional liberal democratic values related to individual freedom coexist with and are reinforced by government institutions which place a high value on individual rights. It is difficult to determine whether it is the values, the government systems which emanate from them, or the interaction of values and institutions which form the most immediate influence on other aspects of US society, but it is clear that together these forces constitute an important systemic influence on American organizations.

Thus, it is apparent that, regardless of the precise nature of the relationship, systemic factors affect the structure of government organizations as well as other types of organization. Second, they influence forms of government intervention and industry response. It is only logical to assume, therefore, that they have an effect upon the individual actions or outcomes of specific organizations.

The combined effect of systemic bias, then, is to constrain the actions of organizations. But because management theory has had considerable difficulty in defining the concept of culture and because the political science literature has focused until recently upon performance in broader terms of the overall political economy of the state, the interrelationship between the factors is still not clear.

The focus of study, then, has been largely on the impact of variations in culture on the structure and internal processes of organizations. Much less attention has been paid to cultural effects on organizational outcomes and performance. This gap in studies of organizations appears to be in large part a result of the variety of disciplines which are interested in the field. Studies on the effect of culture have been primarily carried out by sociologists and others interested in organizational behaviour who tend not to be as interested in outcomes as with the internal dynamic of organizations. Studies related to performance and the effect of structure on outcomes have been in large part carried out by management theorists, predominantly American, who have had less interest in the effect of cultural variations. Political scientists, on the other hand, interested in the relationship between institutions and culture have focused on broad policy outcomes and the behaviour of industry groups rather than individual organization.

The conclusion suggested by all of these studies is that organizations are, in some important ways, culture-bound. The relationship between culture and structure does affect the ways in which the managers of organizations respond to their environment, their technology and the size of their firms. It also affects the values and expectations of most of the participants in the organization, thus influencing management style. The relationship with outcomes or performance is not as well established. There is reason to suspect, however, that variations in structure sometimes result from deliberate attempts to counteract culture, and thus to provide comparable levels of performance.

> The multinational corporation finds out fairly soon that in order to . . . achieve more or less similar results in two socio-culturally different countries, it has to control its operation in them through essentially different managerial structures.
>
> (Weinshall 1977: 394)

The effects of systemic bias are, moreover, likely to persist in the longer term, thus distorting outcomes, because there is no strong countervailing set of values within the organization, and because the example provided by other organizations within the society is likely to be based on the same set of cultural values. Even if the systemic bias has negative consequences for the organization, corrective and adaptive processes may be inadequate because cultural values are often unquestioned, unconscious and almost instinctive within a society. Adaptive capacity may be further limited if the systemic bias towards a particular management style produces a management team that is homogeneous in the relevant values and especially if this management group is able to control the selection of new members.

CONSERVATISM AND ORGANIZATIONAL OUTCOMES

Not all of the values and belief systems of a society would be expected to have a noticeable effect upon the outcomes of organizations within that society. The relevant cultural traits are those which are inconsistent with some course of action which might otherwise be followed by an organization, and which therefore reduce the likelihood that these alternatives will be considered or implemented.

One broad cultural dimension which is particularly relevant to decision-making is the 'conservatism' of the society; that is, the cluster of attitudes and values which indicates a general preference for stability rather than change; a premium on the avoidance of uncertainty; a distaste for risk-taking; and a respect for established authority and deference towards elites (Carroll 1984). Defined in its traditional sense, conservatism is an important factor in organizational decision-making. We know that the 'view of the world' of decision-makers, whether they are pessimistic or optimistic, affects their preferences about decisions, whether they will take risks, and the degree to which they consider the future to be known (Cohen and Cyert 1965: 310). This concept of perceived certainty is central to the decision-making model (Downs 1967).

To the extent that a culture emphasizes values which have a high salience for organizational decision-making, these are also likely to produce a preference for particular types of managers. In countries where consensus is valued, managers who widely consult will be viewed as 'good'. Yet in another country where decisiveness is viewed as a valued trait, the same type of manager could be viewed as 'weak' or bad.

The seminal work in this field is Hofstede's (1980) analysis of the attitudes and values of different cultural groups over a ten year period. He establishes that there are widely varying national patterns of attitudes towards what might be considered as key organizational variables: power distance, uncertainty avoidance, individualism and masculinity. All of these have a clear connection with conservatism. A high level of power distance denotes a respect for authority. A high level of uncertainty avoidance or an unwillingness to take risks may be indicated by a clustering in the ideological centre, and a desire for stability. A high level of individualism is an 'I' orientation, with everyone in society taking care of himself – a form of classical liberalism – rather than society having a collective responsibility, a meaning which comes closer to our contemporary notion of American liberalism. It emphasizes individual decisions, and individual initiative and achievement. Masculinity combines some of the measures for individualism and optimism, but includes measures such as the desire to take individual action, assertiveness and less of a concern with creativity and broader social action.

In relating these values to organizational behaviour and managerial behaviour, Hofstede suggested that a high level of uncertainty avoidance would lead to organizations characterized by consistent management styles; uniformity by standardization; a low turnover of staff; and an emphasis on controlling uncertainty (Hofstede 1980: 176). High power distance was associated with deference towards authority and closely controlled behaviour (ibid.: 119). Alternatively, a high level of individualism would lead to high turnover; fewer rules; a tendency to adopt 'modern' management practices; and promotion from outside rather than on the basis of seniority or internal expertise (ibid.: 238). A high masculinity index would lead to a strong career orientation and an emphasis upon growth with career aspirations taking precedence over other factors such as family or social life (ibid.: 296). Conservatism, therefore would be associated with high levels of power distance and uncertainty avoidance, and low levels of individualism and masculinity.

SYSTEMIC DIFFERENCES BETWEEN CANADA AND THE UNITED STATES

Conservatism is a particularly appropriate focus for research which compares the behaviour of organizations in Canada and the United States. Many people in other countries view the people of these two countries as almost indistinguishable. Yet the difference between the two countries on the dimension of conservatism has been extensively demonstrated empirically, and it is generally accepted that there are fundamental differences in cultural attitudes related to conservatism, with Canadians being more conservative than Americans (Amour and Trott 1981; Bell and Tepperman 1979; Clement 1977; Carroll 1990a; Presthus 1973). The most authoritative author on this subject is Seymour Martin Lipset. His research spans more than three decades and he concludes that there is 'a greater conservatism in Canada', and that 'there can be little doubt that regardless of how much emphasis is placed on structural or cultural (values) factors in accounting for variations, that Canada and the United States continue to differ considerably in this respect' (Lipset 1986: 118, 146).

The impact of these differences in attitudes upon social and political institutions and public policy has also been demonstrated. Goldberg and Mercer (1986), who provide the most extensive review of this literature, have shown how these differences have affected patterns of urban development. Other studies have focused on federalism and regional structures, political parties, constitutional development, and forms of regulation (Gibbins 1982; Nemetz *et al.* 1986; Westin 1983). Both Mintz (1979) and Chase (1986) have also attributed the difference between Canadian and American banking structures to differences in banking regulation which, in Canada, favour elite accommodation and risk-avoidance.

The reflection of these differences within organizations is not as clear. Hofstede's (1980) evidence, for example, supports the general argument that Canadian managers are more conservative. Canadian respondents had a greater desire to avoid uncertainty and placed a lower value upon individualism than those in the US.[3] It should be kept in mind, moreover, that Hofstede's sample was drawn from a multinational corporation which prides itself upon fostering its own internal organizational culture.[4] Other studies that have compared Canadian and American organizations provide additional support for this thesis. Carlisle's (1966) study of the managerial attitudes and practices of American, English-Canadian and French-Canadian managers in one multinational firm operating in Canada found differences which suggest a greater conservatism among Canadians. MacCrimmon and Wehrung (1986), in their extended study of the attitudes towards risk-taking of five hundred managers in Canada and the United

States, also found that executives in both countries perceived Canadians as more risk averse.

While the literature demonstrates a greater conservatism within Canadian organizations, the consequences of this difference are not as clear. MacCrimmon and Wehrung, for example, found no significant differences in performance. McMillan *et al.* (1973) found little difference in structure between Canadian and US firms, although Canadian firms tended to be slightly more formalized. Similarly, despite differences in the regulatory environment, Mintz did not find an appreciable difference in the performance of banks in the two countries. Khandwalla (1977), however, found relationships between the structures of Canadian organizations and their managers' attitudes towards efficiency, growth, innovation, conservatism, democracy, risk-taking and managerial styles, with congruency of values and structure affecting performance. Nightingale (1977) found that differences in values between French- and English-speaking managers affected structure, although he could not derive a significant relationship with performance.

On the whole, then, there are grounds for accepting that there is a more conservative systemic bias in Canada than in the United States, and for believing that this difference in cultural tendencies is reflected in the structure and management styles of organizations in the two countries. What is not clear is whether this instance of systemic bias has significant consequences for organizations. Decision-making processes may differ, but are the outcomes of these processes significantly different? It is one thing to demonstrate that systemic differences exist, but quite another to show that they matter.

Any research dealing with values has difficulty in isolating the independent variables, and this is one of the factors which makes comparisons between Canada and the United States particularly useful. In most cross-cultural studies differences in education and experience are problematic (Jaeger 1982–3). It is never clear whether behavioural differences are a result of systemic factors, or of differences in knowledge and experience. When dealing with business behaviour in Canada and the United States, this becomes less of a problem. Canadians go to Harvard and Stanford business schools with the same enthusiasm as Americans. Even when they do not attend the same universities, they read the same books, watch the same television shows and are taught to a considerable extent by American-trained professors in their universities. The latter is particularly true of Canadian business schools. Of business schools in Canada offering a doctoral degree in the mid-1980s, over 67 per cent of the faculty members had received their highest degree in the United States, and more than 40 per cent had done all of their post-secondary education in the United States.[5] In

Table 4.1 Variables by country (mean levels)

	Canada	USA
Administrative Cost Ratio (ACR) (%)	17	17
Annual change (%) in ACR	0.42	0.43
Size (assets in millions)[a]	$12,760	$11,440
Environment (indicated by % annual change in revenues)	24	24
Performance (indicated by % annual return on revenues)	6	6
Management changes*	8	11
Size of board of directors*	28	13

Notes: The number of firms in the sample is 374.
[a] The size of the organizations is indicated by assets measured in the currency of the country in which they are located.
* Difference is significant at the 0.05 level.
N = 374

the case of Canada and the United States, therefore, it seems safe to assume that knowledge of management practices and the contextual situation is similar in both countries.

A comparative study of similar organizations in Canada and the United States represents a case of 'least difference'.[6] The two countries are similar in many aspects of their cultures, and in their economies. The two economies are also reasonably similar in terms of their levels of development and performance, despite differences in their governmental structures. The systemic differences in degrees of cultural conservatism stand out, then, in these otherwise quite comparable contexts.[7]

The degree to which the firms in the sample are alike can be seen from the mean figures in Table 4.1. Unlike our earlier findings on differences between management types, overall these Canadian and American organizations are strikingly similar on all of the key variables. They have similar administrative cost ratios; they are of similar sizes; and their performances from 1971 to 1982 were roughly the same.

SYSTEMIC DIFFERENCES IN DECISION-MAKING

Given that the United States and Canada have systemic differences in their degree of conservatism we must ask to what extent these differences influence the outcomes and decision-making of organizations in the two countries. When country is added to the model it adds little to its

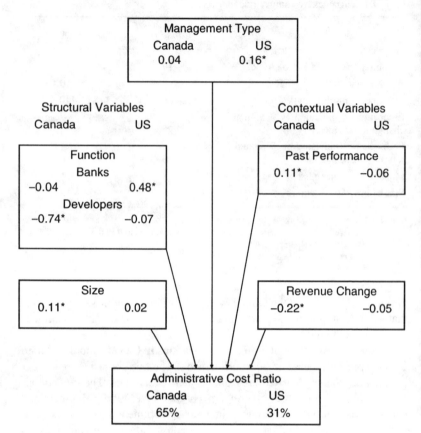

Figure 4.1 The impact of systemic bias on budget decisions
Notes: Relative weight of variables.
    Per cent of variance explained.
    N = 341
    * t-statistic significant at 0.05 level.

explanatory power. The explained variance increases only 1 per cent for both the administrative cost ratio (to 39 per cent) and the change in the level (to 30 per cent). But the addition of country is 'statistically significant'. This means that country is important, but its impact is being felt through its effect on the other factors. The most interesting finding is that while systemic bias adds very little, its inclusion negates the effect of managerial bias found in the last chapter. The relative weight and direction of the other variables remains unchanged, but the significant non-rational variable is now 'country'. If we look at the application of the model on firms in both countries, the pattern is not as clear as it was for differences in management type, but there are differences which are consistent with differences in the degree of systemic conservatism. Conservatism appears to be exhibited in Canadian organizations by a greater degree of predictability, a lack of responsiveness of overhead costs to environmental change, a greater willingness to change variable costs rather than overhead costs, a lesser willingness to change management, and a stronger tendency for environmental scanning and institutional activities.

Perhaps the most central element in the cluster of values that constitute conservatism is a preference for the known and familiar, and an aversion to risk and change. The comparative values for the two countries in our decision-making model are given in Figure 4.1, with the figures on the left giving the Canadian numbers and those on the right the American. In the first place, evidence of Canadian conservatism is shown by the much greater strength of the model in predicting administrative costs decisions at 65 per cent versus 31 per cent for the United States firms. In setting budget levels, Canadian organizations are influenced more by known, objective circumstances and less by managerial idiosyncrasies than in comparable US firms. It would seem that American organizations place a higher value on individualism, and thus permit or encourage managers to take initiatives and, as a consequence, to behave in less predictable ways.

Second, in the Canadian organizations the proportion of the budget that is allocated to administrative costs is influenced by all of the structural and contextual factors. The function of the organization is the most important of these constraints, although firms in the Canadian financial sector behave similarly. Structural and contextual factors have less effect on the level of the administrative cost ratio for the American firms. Management type, however, is relevant for predicting the ACR levels for American firms with administrative managers having a higher level of ACR. This is a finding quite different from the last chapter, where there were lower levels of ACR for administrative managers overall. Except to the degree that American banks differ from the other two industries, management type is the only relevant factor in that country. Canadian firms, on the other hand, behave in a fashion consistent with the rational model irrespective of management type.

In Canada loans and trust companies have similar ACR levels to banks, whereas in the US they are considerably lower. Taken with the relevance of management type in the US firms, this provides additional support for the suggestion in the previous chapter that administrative managers in the savings and loan industries in the US maintain high administrative cost levels.

A further result of differences in conservatism is the difference in our ability to predict change or adaptation as shown in Figure 4.2. American firms appear to be more amenable to change than their Canadian

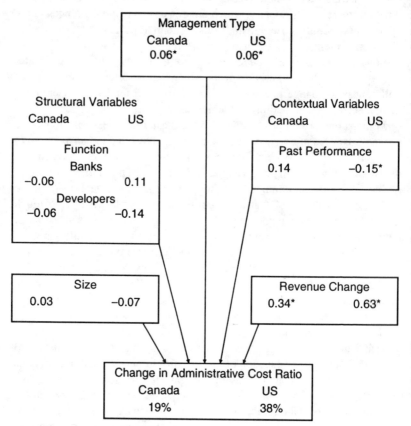

Figure 4.2 The impact of systemic bias on adaptation
Notes: Relative weight of variables.
    Per cent of variance explained.
    N = 341
    * t-statistic significant at 0.05 level.

counterparts, which seem to prefer stability.[8] Moreover, the response of Canadian firms to changes in previous performance levels is in the opposite direction to that of US companies. A decline in profit levels in the Canadian firms coincides with a reduction or no change in the level of their ACR, while among the American firms the same decline in performance produces an increase in the ratio of administrative costs to total expenditures. This is consistent with the risk-aversion behaviour expected of Canadian managers. There is also an independent difference in the effect of management type in the US although it has no effect in Canada. In fact, after the

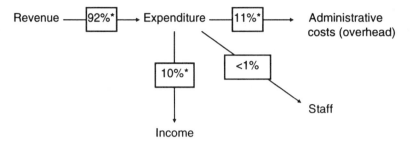

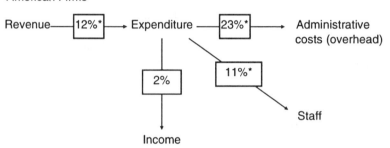

Figure 4.3 Paths of decision-making
Notes: Statistics are r-square values showing the percentage of the variation in the rates of
     change of pairs of variables which can be statistically explained.
     * t-statistic significant at 0.05 level.

functional difference of banks – management type is the most important
variable in explaining budgetary levels in the US firms.

   The decision path analysis also shows differences. When adjusting overall
expenditure levels, the Canadian firms seem to respond to changes in revenue
levels (92 per cent) to a much greater degree than the American firms (12 per
cent). But there is almost no corresponding change in administrative costs or
staffing in Canada (11 per cent and 0) – changes in expenditure are concentrated in the production portions of the firm. Both of these findings are
consistent with a greater desire for stability in Canada, and they may also
reflect a more entrenched administrative structure in Canadian firms, which is
consistent with greater conservatism. The American firms seem to base
changes in expenditures on some factor other than changes in revenues. When
expenditures do change, however, this change tends to be more concentrated
on administrative costs and staff. Overall, the outcome of this confounding

effect is that year-to-year variations in revenue have about the same impact on the administrative cost ratio in Canada and the US. As change in revenue is the only relevant factor influencing the American firms to change their ACR, this confirms the somewhat idiosyncratic appearance of the budgetary patterns in the US firms and a more balanced or rationally determined approach on the part of Canadian firms.

In the Canadian organizations, the proportion of the budget that is allocated to administrative costs is determined by both structural and contextual factors. The level of the administrative cost ratio for the American firms is less predictable and varies by management type. And yet these same American managers react more strongly to environmental change than do their Canadian counterparts. As variations in economic conditions alter the revenue of an organization, American managers respond more directly by changing the administrative cost ratio than do Canadian companies that experience similar environmental disturbances. Canadian firms change their expenditures more dramatically, but do so in a way that preserves the existing ratio of administrative to production costs. The overall effect is that the performance of the organizations in the two countries remains approximately the same over time but their actions differ in ways that are consistent with their differing degrees of systemic bias in the form of conservatism.

Management stability and boundary-scanning

Two important factors influencing organizational adaptation are the ability to perceive a problem or a change in the environment and the ability to change the makeup of the management group to include those best able to deal with the problem. The rational model suggests that one means of perceiving change and correcting for bias is to enlarge the boundary-scanning component of the organization (Downs 1967; Thompson 1967). In Chapter 3 no relationship was found to exist between management type and management change. But the effects of conservatism should produce a systemic difference in both management change and boundary-spanning. In the last section we found that Canadian firms had a tendency not to change staff levels. Following from this it would be expected that Canadian firms would also have a more entrenched management structure. It would also follow that, in order to be able to recognize changes in the environment, they would put a higher priority on boundary scanning activities.

Stability of management was measured in two ways: the absolute amount of change in membership in the senior management group, and the frequency of change in management type. (Changes in management type occur when there are sufficient changes in management to alter the sub-system balance of

Table 4.2 Management changes and size of board of directors

	Size of board of directors		Management changes	
	Mean	*Adjusted eta-square*	*Mean*	*Adjusted eta-square*
Overall	23.4		9.5	
Country				
Canada	31.3		8.0	
US	15.0		10.9	
		0.42		0.16
Function				
Banks				
Canada	42.8		6.0	
US	20.6		13.4	
Loan companies				
Canada	28.8		8.6	
US	11.0		10.4	
Developers				
Canada	13.5		9.3	
US	7.6		9.8	
		0.49		<0.01
r-square (Country and Function)	0.83			0.18

the management group.) Actual changes in management were more frequent in the US, although the difference is fairly small (Table 4.2). Nevertheless country can explain 16 per cent of the difference in the number of management changes between the two countries.[9] The average number of changes were greater for all types of companies in the US. The smallest difference is in the development companies which were more likely to be owner-managed in the United States. There were also more changes in management type in the United States (twelve) than in Canada (eight).

A related phenomenon, which was not measured but was notable, was movement between firms in the same industry. This 'company hopping' was predicted by Hofstede (1980) who found many US respondents who did not expect to stay with the company for more than two years, reinforcing his finding of a higher level of individualism. A representative of one of the Canadian development companies, when discussing the problems which ensued when Canadian firms hired Americans when entering the US markets, observed that, 'they [Americans] had no company feeling. They were just out for themselves. You can call it individualism, I would be more inclined to think them a bunch of crooks.' Schull and Gibson (1982: 68), in their history of the Bank of Nova Scotia, had to go back to the nineteenth century to give examples of bank hopping. Yet three such cases were noted in the American banks during the period of this study, and the sample consisted of only five out of some 15,000 American banks. In the period since this study took place there has been an increase in the 'company-hopping' in Canada as changes in regulations and rationalization prompted many loan companies to amalgamate and increase their geographic coverage. As a result, a number of senior bank executives have moved into the loan company sector, but not to different banks.[10]

Organizations can try to reduce uncertainty and predict changes in the environment through boundary scanning activities. An important vehicle for such activities is the board of directors. The degree to which boundary scanning is emphasized or carried out, therefore, can be measured by the size of the board of directors of the organization. The average size of the board for Canadian companies was 31.3 compared to 15.0 for the American sample. These differences were consistent for all types of companies, and country accounts for 42 per cent of the difference in the size of the boards.

The effect of function is also evident, with an eta-square of 0.49. Together, country and function account for 83 per cent of the difference in the size of the boards of directors. The banking sector provides an indication of the extent to which such behaviour is institutionalized. American banks are limited by law to a maximum of 25 board members. Nevertheless, the average within the sample is only 20.6, well below the maximum. The average in Canada is 42.8.[11]

CONCLUSION

In this chapter we have found that overall Canadian firms are more predictably sensitive to structural and contextual factors in their decision-making while US firms tend to be more idiosyncratic. We also found the preference for stability that is typical of conservatism will produce a more entrenched administrative structure and a stronger sense of technological determinism among Canadian firms. Finally, the desire for stability led to fewer management changes in Canada while the greater sensitivity to the environment led to a larger boundary spanning role.

The impact of systemic bias within organizations has been explained as 'employment practices and organizational arrangements that come to be culturally accepted and defined as good . . . [but] these properties need not have any close correspondence to efficiency or technical rationality' (Pfeffer 1982: 251–2). Thus, correspondence with cultural norms is often considered irrelevant to the needs of technical efficiency. But the impact of systemic bias is important, not only for individual firms, but also for the overall performance of an economy. Zysman (1983) has shown how the structure of domestic institutions determines how external disturbances are translated and responded to as *domestic* disturbances. In turn, this affects individual behaviour, with firms adapting through shifts in resource patterns. Thus, there are two effects of bias – the institutional response and the individual firm's response.

We have seen that two such practices or arrangements – the willingness to change management or administrative costs and the emphasis upon boundary scanning and response to the environmental changes – are different in Canada and the United States. In the two countries, therefore, there appear to be differences in the patterns of organizational adaptation. But the degree of success of adaptation as measured by the performance of the firms does not vary. (Admittedly, the tests within this study deal with after tax rather than before tax income figures, and it is possible that a society that does not value risk will not reward it in its tax system.)

Cultural values, such as those associated with conservatism, differentiate one culture from another and set parameters for their institutions and political systems. Because these values are held by most of the individuals within a society, they are also held by most or all of the people within organizations in that society, and thus act to differentiate organizations in one culture from those in another. To the extent, then, that organizations are constrained in their actions by these values and the institutional and political structures which reflect them, we have a systemic source of organizational bias. While alternative values imported from other countries may partly counterbalance the systemic effects, they are likely to be too diffused or too weak to fully overcome the stronger, more widely held values.

Finding systemic biases consistent with the differing degrees of conservatism in these two countries, therefore, may have broader implications. Canada and the United States are considered to be part of the grouping of Western liberal, primarily Anglo-American, countries. Thus, while they differ on all of the measures of conservatism charted by Hofstede (1980), there are large numbers of countries which are far more conservative. Islamic countries, for example, are noted for being conservative (Carroll 1984). Most of the countries in the European Community are more conservative in terms of their uncertainty avoidance and individualism; while the countries of the Pacific Rim (with the exception of Australia and New Zealand) tend also to be more conservative on all measures. If we want to understand decision-making in firms on a broader basis, we must keep in mind that cultural values will have an effect. To the degree that there is interaction between managerial and systemic bias, developing practices consistent with the prevailing degree of conservatism may be even more relevant in management and design prescriptions intended to bridge cultural boundaries than would be the case if systemic bias were the only constraint. It is to those interaction effects that I turn next.

5   Management type, performance and viability

INTRODUCTION

The last two chapters have shown that the rational model of decision-making is improved when systematic short-term bias is incorporated by the inclusion of specific and measurable non-rational factors. We have seen that organizations and their managements are biased in a fashion consistent with the systemic values of the country of which the organization is a part; and in a fashion consistent with the values of the sub-system from which the management group emanate. While factors such as size, technology, the environment, and the response to past performance are important in predicting outcomes, they are more important in some countries and for some types of management than others.

   In this chapter we turn to three questions which arise from these results. The systemic value tested was 'conservatism' – the preference for stability, and a dislike for taking risks. While this factor was found to be important, the degree of uncertainty avoidance was also found to be high among the administrative managers – those whose background and training was in the managerial or control sub-system of the organization. This raises the question of the extent to which there is an interactive effect between the two forms of bias.

   Second, my emphasis so far has been on the decision outcomes or preferences of the management group. We have considered the extent to which the existence and continuation in power of a particular management group can lead the organization to consider only certain alternatives when faced with a problem. As resource allocation is one of the most important factors in organizational behaviour, the impact of systemic factors and management type on budget allocations has been explored. But if there is to be any prescriptive element to these findings, they must be related to organizational performance and viability. While we know that management type affects preferences, does it affect the performance of the organization and, in particular, does it affect performance differently in differing types of environments? When times are good, management type and bias may not be important, but in an unfavourable environment the existence of bias, or a bias which could reduce performance, can undermine the long-term viability of the organization.

This brings us to the final question. Is there an 'ideal' management type, one which might be considered to be unbiased and successful under any environmental or systemic condition? This last point is of particular relevance because it could solve the problem of constantly trying to change the management of the organization to 'catch up' to changes in the environment. In effect, such a management configuration would have a continuing, inherent ability to bring about organizational adaptation to environmental change.

INTERACTION, PERFORMANCE AND VIABILITY

The interaction of systemic and managerial bias

The findings in Chapter 3 confirmed the existence of managerial sub-system dominance and managerial bias. While only two of the possible configurations of management outlined in Chapter 1 were considered – the specific cases of managerial biases which favour either the administrative or technical sub-systems of the organization – there were differences evident in the allocation of funds to administrative and managerial activities as opposed to operational or technical activities. There was a preference for administrative managers to emphasize stability and control and for technical managers to have a greater propensity to change and to favour production solutions. Administrative type managers emphasizing control on average spent a lower proportion of expenditures on administrative costs. They did, however, show a lower propensity to change the ratio of administrative costs to total expenditures and had higher rates of increase in their overhead costs. More importantly, there was a notable difference in overall performance between the two types of management.

But when systemic bias was taken into consideration the effect of managerial bias was considerably weakened, despite there being no correlation between management type and country, nor among management type, country and function. This suggests that there is an interactive effect between management type and country.

In order to test for this interaction we can look at each of the four variations of management configurations separately – Canadian/technical, Canadian/administrative, American/technical and American/administrative. We began in Chapter 1 by being able to explain 17 per cent of the variation in the year-to-year administrative cost levels for all organizations. Adding two forms of non-rational bias improved this to 38 per cent. When we look

Table 5.1 The model and interaction

	Canadian technical	Canadian administrative	American technical	American administrative
ACR				
r = square (%)	62	76	44	31
Change in ACR				
r = square (%)	30	16	39	45
Mean level ACR	18	16	18	16
Percentage correlation in rate of change of:				
Revenue: Expenditures	92	91	90	45
After-tax profit	7.6	4.5	7.2	5.1
N =	113	72	111	63

at the four separate management configurations considered the model improves even more dramatically. We now can account for as much as 76 per cent of the variation for Canadian/administrative managers, 62 per cent for Canadian/technical managers, 44 per cent for American/technical managers but only 31 per cent for American/administrative managers.

Similarly, the model originally accounted for only 6 per cent of differences in the rates of change in ACR – our measure of adaptation. It has improved for each of the four management configurations, and the pattern for change is exactly the opposite for that of administrative costs generally. Among American/administrative managers, we can explain 45 per cent of the change in administrative costs, 39 per cent for American/ technical managers, 30 per cent for Canadian/technical managers and only 16 per cent for Canadian administrative managers.

For Canadian managers we are better able to explain the level of administrative costs, and for American managers the willingness to change these costs. But within each category the interaction of management type seems to alter this pattern. For technical managers, in Canada we can explain less of the variance in administrative costs, for American technical managers more. In terms of adaptation for American technical managers we can explain less of the variance and for Canadian technical managers more.

For American administrative managers, the pattern may be a function of a tendency on their part to act in idiosyncratic ways, and to be unaware of, or ignore, the industry norms. Their tendency towards risk-taking produces a greater degree of volatility. Technical management, on the other hand, may represent an ameliorating effect.

The idiosyncratic nature of the American/administrative managers can also be seen with respect to the decision-path. While for three types of management configuration changes in revenues can explain 90 per cent or more of variations in changes in expenditures, for the American/administrative managers it is less than 50 per cent – indicating that changes in revenue and expenditure move quite independently of each other for firms of this type.

If being able to explain how managers act is our goal, this interaction between the two forms of bias raises the possibility that the management type which is prefered in one country may not be preferable in another. The form of management which reduces levels of risk-taking and increases control (i.e. administrative type management) may be beneficial in some countries as a means of controlling systemic individualism, but harmful in those where systemic conservatism exists. The confidence managers gain from having a firmly based functional expertise could justify their taking risks – making technical managers preferable in countries with high levels of conservatism. Similarly the 'modern management techniques' of administrative managers might act to counteract the individualism of a less conservative systemic bias.

While few studies of preferences for particular management types have been done in Canada, those which do exist show that for a long period of time technical management was predominant in banking, construction, and mining (Clement 1977; Goldenberg 1981; Schull and Gibson 1982). Even when technical managers were not specifically sought, the stability of management led them to develop and act in a similar fashion as they adopted the culture of their company and industry. On the other hand, the propensity for American companies to hire and promote those with general management rather than function specific skills has also been well documented (Reich 1983; Thompson 1976). It would appear, then, that there may be a natural or rational tendency to promote the type of manager who could counteract the less desirable systemic attributes to produce an overall 'ideal'.

The interaction between management type and culture also suggests that prescriptions for success are more likely to work if they explicitly recognize the dominant systemic influences on the firm. The success in some cases, and failure in others, of attempts to accommodate Japanese management practices in Canadian and American firms can be attributed to the recognition, or non-recognition, of the fact that there are incompatible systemic biases which must be overcome (Baar and Tomako 1988).

Much of the concern in Canadian economic policy in the past two decades has centred upon the unwillingness or inability of business to capitalize upon development opportunities and take risks without government support. This has resulted in many of the high risk/high payoff industries being foreign-owned. Solutions to the 'Canadian' problem tend to follow a convergence theory, advocating the adoption of American prescriptive theories in terms of either structure or managerial style. One example is the *Royal Commission on Corporate Concentration in Canada*, which concludes that 'Canadian firms have been characterized by inadequate R&D, innovation and export performance and perhaps risk-taking compared with firms in the same industry in other countries' (Canada 1978: 213). Most of the comparison was with United States firms. But it is possible that what they are saying, in fact, is that Canadians are too inclined to act like Canadians. The form of management which may reduce levels of risk-taking and increase control (i.e. administrative type management) may be beneficial in the United States but harmful in Canada.

For example, William Mulholland, who was head of the Canadian Bank of Montreal for part of this study (1975–81), was both an American and an administrative manager, and his actions stand out as an example of both forms of bias. He is credited with reorganizing the bank's internal operations, yet he also took the risky strategy of expanding more than the other Canadian banks into Third World lending. It should be noted that five years after his take-over, the bank's profit margins were lower than its competitors (Stoffman 1989). The performance of the other Canadian bank which had administrative management remained good throughout the period of the study, but by the late 1980s had fallen off. In 1990 the senior management was changed and the new head of the bank is a technical manager, which should produce a more balanced management.

The existence of bias may also have important implications for the impact of 'free trade' in the two countries.[1] Companies which have successfully structured themselves, and adopted a management type which is amenable to the systemic requirements of one country may find that they do not operate as successfully in the other country, particularly if they are also operating with management who do not share the systemic values of the country in which they are now competing. One of the reasons for the success of the Japanese is they have used North American marketing firms to sell their goods in North America while producing them in their own country or in other countries with which they shared values. When they began to manufacture goods in North America they adapted their structures and management styles to conform to the changed systemic environment.

The early lack of success of Canadian developers in the United States market may be another example of this problem. Highly successful firms such as Cadillac-Fairview, Campeau and Nu-West, all with technical management types at the time, suffered setbacks when they entered the United States markets in the late 1970s. Whether the actual managers were American or Canadian made no difference. In the former case, the company did not understand the style of the managers; in the latter, they were unable to react to environmental shifts. Only when Cadillac-Fairview changed to an administrative management type did it begin to succeed in the United States. It should be noted, however, that in doing this they also moved out of the residential development business in Canada.

The experience of Labatts may underline the problem of interactive bias. A Canadian brewing and entertainment giant, it expanded into the dairy industry in both Canada and the United States in the early 1980s. It was not a successful venture. While the Canadian dairy division has been moderately profitable, the US operation never did well – 'almost profitable' is the best company officials would ever say about it. They came to recognize that the technical requirements of the dairy industry were different from those of their basic industry, 'different businesses with different operational needs'. In the US this problem was magnified by the environment, 'Labatt didn't expect competition to be so brutal' in the US (Bertin 1992; Feschuk 1992). They have since divested themselves of the dairy operations and 'gone back to our roots'. While managerial bias in Canada was overcome and the firm was moderately (but not over-whelmingly) profitable – the addition of the systemic factor in the US produced unprofitability.

Overall, therefore, both managerial and systemic bias affect the *means* by which decisions are made. By including these non-rational factors in the model of decision-making, the decision process becomes more predictable. But being able to predict management decisions is not our only goal. Inevitably, the test of the success of management is, to a large extent, its ability to achieve acceptable performance levels and maintain the viability of the organization. While there were differences in performance between the two types of management there was no difference between firms in the two countries.

Relationship to performance and viability

When performance among the four types of management is compared, technical managers in Canada had the highest level of overall profit, at 7.6 per cent, followed by technical management in the US, at 7.2 per cent. The administrative managers are lower, with American/administrative manage-ment at 5.1 per cent and Canadian/administrative management at 4.5 per cent. Overall, technical managers do better in both countries but the variation is much greater in Canada. On the other hand, the idiosyncratic behaviour of American/administrative managers does not seem to hurt their balance sheets to the same degree. The level of ACR for the four management types also shows that low administrative costs do not necessarily produce higher levels of profits.

Do these patterns persist regardless of variation in environmental conditions? Bias could be evident in outcomes during times of expansion, or in a favourable environment, but it would be less likely to create serious problems under such circumstances because in good times there is likely to be sufficient slack within organizations to overcome its effects. Bias becomes a problem in times of contraction, when resources are tight, as rapid change makes it more important that the organization be able to scan all of the environment and not just a part of it.

The existence of differing environmental conditions throws additional light on our findings about overall performance. During good times in which the firms were experiencing growth, the administrative managers performed better with an average profit level that was half a percentage point higher than that of technical managers.[2] Given that the overall average profit level during good times was 7.9 per cent, this translates into a 6 per cent performance margin in favour of administrative managers. The opposite is true when times were bad because of an unfavourable environment. Technical managers performed better by an absolute amount of 0.80 per cent. As the average profit level during bad times was 4.5 per cent, this produces a 19 per cent performance margin in favour of technical managers. When these differences are further broken down by country, there is very little difference between the two types of Canadian managers under either environmental condition. That is, while technical managers do better in a negative environment and administrative managers in a favourable environment, the variation between them is not great. This is not the case in the US. In good times the administrative managers do slightly better than the technical managers. In an unfavourable environment, however, the difference becomes quite dramatic – for administrative managers in fact often lose money.

An illustration of this difference is evident in the profit levels of firms in the US savings and loan industry. All six of the firms studied had high levels of profits from 1972 to 1979. Beginning in 1979, as they moved into the recession, the profit levels for each of the firms fell quite precipitously. Significantly, the three firms with administrative management all showed negative profit levels for at least one of the next three years.

We have seen that while administrative management is more profitable in a favourable environment, technical representation is more profitable in an unfavourable environment. Thompson suggested that in an uncertain environment the technical core should be represented in the dominant coalition. To the extent that performance can be considered a measure of his hypothesis, it seems to be supported. Finally, we have seen that if we wish to provide for differing environmental conditions it would appear that on average technical management will perform better, but the differences between the two types of management type are greater in Canada than in the United States. Alternatively, the management may change, or be changed, to reflect the needs of the changing environment.

But simply changing managers is not enough. The relationship between the number of management changes and performance (after-tax return on revenue) was negative, although quite weak (r-square = 2 per cent). Thus firms with large numbers of management changes tended to have lower levels of performance than those with stable management. What is required is not only changes in the personnel of the management group, but also changes in managerial type, possibly through a reforming of the coalition by the key stakeholders. This could occur in cases where the organization was faced with a number of continuing crises, or where a severe jolt forced a reassessment of the situation. It did happen in several development companies and banks as a result of the turbulent environment in the late 1970s, including heavy financial losses and ownership changes.[3] It may also have been a factor in the ability of the Continental-Illinois Bank to continue to function. After its financial difficulties in 1984, it returned to a technical management type, as did First Chicago Bank after it experienced a fall-off in profitability.

But, in order for management change to be effective, not only must the 'new' managers represent a different form of bias, but it must be a bias which is consistent with the needs of the environment. Nu-West construction, which had been doing well under technical management during the 'boom' times of the 1970s, switched to administrative management just as the environment became unfavourable and subsequently faced serious financial difficulties.[4]

The goal of firms is not only to make a profit, but to survive. Is there a management pattern which is more likely to provide long term viability or survival? While administrative management may be more profitable during times of prosperity – presumably one would hope that the firm could survive an economic downturn in order to prosper again in the next period of economic growth. The experience of these companies since 1982 can tell us a great deal about the relationship between management type and organizational survival. The general pattern is similar to that which we have already found. Firms with technical management tended to have better survival rates during the recessions of 1980–2 and 1990–2, but those with administrative management had better performance levels during the 1980s.

While none of the banks have failed regardless of management type, the Continental Illinois bank did experience some rather dramatic difficulties, the Marine Midland bank is now controlled by offshore interests, and Bankers Trust has left the retail banking business. Those which had the most difficulty had administrative management and a return to technical management tended to precede improvement. Only four of the six Canadian trust companies are intact as they were, although none failed. Of the US savings and loans companies, two which had administrative management in 1982 subsequently failed. The three with technical management and one with administrative management have remained in business. Notably, the one with administrative management grew to be a nationally based company by the end of the 1980s.

Technical competence seems to be almost essential in deposit-taking firms. There were twenty-two failures of trust companies in Canada between 1980 and 1988, and two bank failures, the first banks to fail since 1922. Although ostensibly the cause of failure was falling real estate markets and, in some cases, too high a dependency upon energy loans, these failures raise the question of why these companies in particular failed when others did not. The failures prompted three government inquiries into their causes.[5] One thing the companies had in common was closely held or individual ownership. But as we saw in Chapter 3, this was in itself not a sufficient explanation for managerial bias. A second attribute each of the companies had in common was an administrative type management with no experience in the business of financial institutions, and who exhibited a remarkable lack of concern with risk assessment, matching rates and the other technical components of deposit-taking.

The inquiry into the failure of the Canadian Commercial Bank noted that it 'suffered during much of its existence from a shortage of senior management personnel experienced in banking', and attributed its collapse to the 'quality of its loan portfolio which in turn was the product of policies adopted by an inexperienced management' (Estey 1986: 3). The failures of the thirteen interlinked companies of Crown, Seaway and Greymac Trust were attributed in part to the owners having 'little interest in the trust business aspect of the companies' (Morrison 1983: 20). Along with failure to meet a number of legal requirements, one of the significant causes of the collapse of the companies was 'management lacking in depth and competence' (ibid.: 110) and the fact that the officers of the company 'had little knowledge and understanding of many of the transactions in which the companies were engaged and that no serious efforts were made to upgrade their level of knowledge or expertise' (ibid.: 204). While these examples are perhaps extreme, what they had in common was a complete lack of representation of the technical sub-system within their management. The one exception to this pattern is the failure of the Principal Trust group of companies. In this case there was technical representation through the owner and chief executive officer, but this is an instance in which criminal charges of fraud were later laid.

Returning to our sample, two of the Canadian developers left the construction business after the 1980 recession. Two others almost failed in subsequent years, and both had administrative management. One of these firms had experienced a management change from technical to administrative, a change which coincided with a shift to an unfavourable environment – the 1980 recession.[6] The other survived the recession but left the industry after having been bought, as part of a bailout, by a non-development firm. A fifth changed ownership, switched to an administrative management during the 1980s, and prospered. It is now in severe financial difficulty, however, as a result of overbuying land in the late 1980s prior to the 1990–2 recession. One firm with technical management remains healthy and intact. All but one of the US development companies are still in business, although three had ownership changes. Only one, which had administrative management, subsequently failed – U.S. Home filed for bankruptcy protection in 1990.

This is not proof, of course, of a causal link between management type and viability – the firms could have all undergone changes in management type in the years after this study ended. But if I was putting my long term investment money on the balance of probabilities, I would have a preference, or bias, for firms with technical management. The problem, of course, is that I might have to accept a lower level of return during times of economic growth.

The lessons we have drawn to this point are that management type does matter, perhaps more so in the United States than in Canada, and, in particular, it matters in an unfavourable environment. This raises the third question to be addressed in this chapter – is there one type of management configuration or sub-system representation which can be considered to be the 'ideal'; one which would be successful across a more diverse amalgam of companies and systemic values, and in both favourable and unfavourable environmental conditions?

THE 'IDEAL' MANAGEMENT TYPE

Those sub-systems which should be represented within the management group are those best able to handle the 'critical contingencies', the problems the organization faces. It is possible, therefore, to specify circumstances in which it is clear that representation from a particular sub-system is desirable. It is even possible, as we have done, to specify circumstances in which dominance by one sub-system might be desirable. The problem of domination, however, is that barring the existence of some omnipotent and omniscient invisible hand which has the power to change the management, it tends to preclude the organization from adapting when a different type of management is required.

In cases where technical problems exist, where a poorly understood technology is in use, where rapid technological change is taking place, or where the technology is non-routine, technical representation is desirable. Examples would include the early days of the computer industry; the banking industry, which went through rapid technological changes during the 1970s; and the construction industry with its non-routine technology (Carroll 1986, 1987).

Institutional representation is required in a highly competitive market, or in an environment which is volatile, such as the airline industry in the period following deregulation. This sub-system would also need to be represented in situations where there is tight coupling between the organization and some outside organization which could control it, as is true of highly regulated industries and companies which are closely held but not owner-managed. Institutional representation is vital to firms of all types during times of economic upheaval, such as when major contractions in the economy are underway.

Finally, managerial specialists are especially important during the levelling off stage after a period of rapid growth, when co-ordination and control problems related to consolidation come to the fore. They tend not to be as helpful during a period of decline, however, as they are inclined to reduce the technical and institutional components of the organization (Laband 1976).

It is also possible to consider the consequences of the bias that results from ignoring one of the sub-systems by having a management that represents only two of the sub-systems. If the institutional segment is ignored, market share could be lost or unfavourable regulations put into place. If the technical sub-system is ignored, product quality and development would not be emphasized. If the managerial system is ignored, problems of co-ordination and control could result.

In different types of circumstances, then, different types of managerial configurations would be desirable. But, as was discussed in Chapter 1, the reality of organizational action and the impact of both previous bias and structural hysteresis make it likely that in only a few, special types of circumstances – such as the existence of an external owner, or the rare brilliance of a gifted management – will the organization shift to meet new management requirements. We are left, then, with trying to identify the most desirable form of management configuration – the one which has the highest probability of meeting most, or at least more, of the critical contingencies facing organizations.

In a favourable environment most organizations are viable, but when the environment becomes unfavourable the structural design and managerial configuration of the organization may be the difference between success and failure. As the main goal of most of the members of any organization is for the organization to survive as a viable and successful entity, it is appropriate to focus on the management configuration which is most useful in an unfavourable environment. While this configuration will not necessarily improve the performance of organizations during good times, it is likely to ensure viability in any type of environmental condition.

We can assume that all members of the organization want it to succeed. Survival may be sufficient to meet the interests of the people running the organization, or perhaps working for it, but it is not always the main goal of other participants. When the value of outstanding stocks is less than the break-up value of the firm, stockholders may prefer it to be sold off in pieces. When the organization is a drain on the resources of the parent company, or of a government, its owners may prefer to kill it off. A goal of survival at any cost, regardless of performance, is in itself a manifestation of managerial bias.

Any reader of the business pages can name a number of high-flying firms, the darlings of management writers and analysts in the 1970s, which did not survive the recession of the early 1980s. The stock brokerage firms and savings and loans companies which were the darlings of the 1980s are now history. No doubt there are others doing well at the moment which will be casualties of the next recession. Even Chrysler Corporation, whose turnaround by Lee Iaccoca made him one of the management gurus of the 1980s, has not been exempt from problems. Iaccoca's 'mea culpa' about the source of a recent problem is relevant: 'If I made one mistake it was delegating all the product development.' He goes on to point out that he had over-emphasized finance and marketing (Taylor 1988: 81).

What is the best management type?

I would now like to consider which type of representation is necessary within most organizations. Very few organizations operate in an environment which is stable and homogeneous. Those which do could survive without institutional representation. The problem, of course, is that the organization without institutional representation or knowledge – like the buggy whip factories at the beginning of this century – may not recognize environmental change when it is upon them.

In addition, the increased role of government in allocating resources and regulating economic life indicates that there almost always are some institutional legitimation responsibilities – to the point that government regulators frequently force such representation through requirements for outside directors. Within the public sector, of course, this need is even greater. The need for broad public acceptability, as well as such issues as the representativeness of the civil service, the need for equity, and the public demand for accountability by both elected and appointed officials, are the institutional concerns of public organizations. Indeed, the Irangate scandal, and earlier problems of the CIA, in the United States can be considered to be a product of organizations or organizational components so concerned with the technical aspects of their goals that they become divorced from the institutional requirements.

Second, the size, diversity of tasks and conflicting goals of most complex organizations also suggest that the managerial sub-system should be represented to deal with control and co-ordination activities. Given that PODSCORB (planning, organizing, directing, staffing, co-ordinating, reporting and budgeting) is the accepted acronym for the functions of the managerial or senior administrative echelons of organizations, and in various formats is the major concern of business schools and managerial training programmes, it is almost inconceivable that this sub-system should not be represented in any organization bigger than a 'mom and pop' store.

Finally, there is the case of representation of the technical sub-system. It requires representation in those cases in which the technology of the organization is imperfect or complex. Firms which have a simple and stable technology could probably function without technical representation, but they would then be unable to detect when changes in technology eventually become required. This could be viewed as the major problem of the 'Big Three' US automobile companies during the 1970s. Automobile technology had ceased to be stable, but they were unable to detect either the technical needs for change or the institutional demands for change because the management had become divorced not only from their markets, but from car production itself (Halberstrom 1986).

Managers are expected to use their judgement in running the organization. Judgement, however, requires knowledge – not just information (Lindblom and Cohen 1958) – and this implies an ability to evaluate the information received. In order for the critical contingencies facing the organization to be recognized, evaluated and resolved there should be someone within the senior management able to evaluate information relating to each of the sub-systems, and to deal with problems of legitimation, technology or control. A lack of technical representation within senior management lies behind Stout's (1980) finding of a tendency towards control over management (or the exercise of judgement). If you do not understand the technology you are working with – that is, if you cannot interpret the information you are given – the exercise of judgement becomes impossible, leaving reliance upon control as the only possible decision strategy. Similarly, Mintzberg's (1988) call for wisdom rather than knowledge, to let those not in senior management levels but deep within the organization deal with problems, is a call for restoring technical competance in decision-making within the organization.

Lack of technical representation can also be a source of problems in take-overs and mergers. These organizations are expanding and moving into new technical areas in which they have no expertise. They may have built up their managerial and institutional capabilities to plan and finance the take-over, but they may or may not have a technical capacity among the old management of the organization that is taken over. If there is a technical capacity within the old management, and it was not a lack of technical management which led to the take-over or merger, and if this source of expertise is maintained, the management will be strengthened. If the old management is hostile to the take-over or is forced to leave, however, the firm is likely to face problems in the near future. Changing the management, therefore, is not always the best solution. Diversified conglomerates, particularly those which have developed slowly, will tend not to experience this problem. The divisionalized, decentralized nature of this form of organizations is more likely to keep a strong technical component in place.

I conclude, therefore, that the 'ideal' is the organization with a balanced management configuration with representation from each of the three subsystems. Institutional and managerial representation are more likely to be present, as there are frequently regulatory requirements for the former and, at least in North America, a cultural inclination for representation of the latter sub-system. It is technical representation which may be most frequently overlooked, and yet it is this role which frequently is the most critical for long term viability. It is the technical sub-system which is concerned with what it is that organizations do.

CONCLUSION

March and Simon point out that 'the world tends to be perceived by the organization's members in terms of the particular concepts that are reflected in the organization's vocabulary' (March and Simon 1958: 165). It follows, then, that the organization also tends to be perceived by its members in terms of the particular concepts reflected in their collective vocabularies and those aspects of the organization's vocabulary with which they are familiar. The standard rational model recognizes bias, but assumes it is individually – rather than socially or structurally – based. Thus, it does not consider patterns of bias which could 'skew' the entire organization and leave it unable to recognize or correct error.

We have seen how the outcomes of organizations are affected by the existence of managerial bias within the organization. Differences in organizational outcomes and in rates of adaptation can be explained in part by viewing the composition of the management group as an independent variable; a non-rational component of the decision-making process.

The existence of managerial bias affects both the goals and the decision-making process of the organization. It exists when one sub-system of the organization comes to dominate the management, and the technology of that sub-system determines the way in which operational goals are defined and choices are made. Bias can be viewed as an overall case of goal displacement in that the goal perceptions of one sub-system become the ends of the organization, and the goal of long term viability may be given insufficient weight.

Bias affects the ability of the organization to adapt, thus reducing the chance of errors being recognized. If there is no source of bias correction within the management structure, communications, search and problem definition will reflect a biased perception of causality. The tendency for uncertainty absorption within the organization then acts to reinforce the existing patterns. Even replacing the managers themselves may not have any effect if the 'new' management represent the same biases as the old, or if the behaviour is rooted in strongly held and unquestioned cultural traits.

The ideal solution to bias is to develop a management group which is balanced, one which includes representation from each of the three sub-systems. This would allow the organization to capitalize upon the benefits of administrative management in good times, and technical management during times of poor economic performance. In addition, the existence of an institutional component would provide the organization with opportunities for environmental scanning. The problem of adaptation would thus be resolved and the impact of systemic bias – if not eliminated – could at least be reduced.

One advantage of studying a small group of firms over time is that it enables us to consider them under varying environmental conditions. The problem, of course, is that this may distort the findings in some way which is idiosyncratic to these particular firms or industries. This may be particularly problematic with the industries studied here because one of them – the development industry – is highly volatile; another – the banking industry – can be considered to be almost insensitive to environmental change; while the third – the loans industry – experienced an unusually high level of volatility during the period of the study. In addition, the industries were selected in part because they have a high degree of technological determinism. This may be the reason why the firms in the sample demonstrated almost complete single sub-system domination, and it may be why it was impossible to consider the independent effect of institutional representation. In the next chapter we consider the impact of other forms of management types across a broader range of industries in order to consider the extent to which this model of managerial bias can explain more general variations of managerial behaviour.

6 The bias of management

INTRODUCTION

I have focused thus far on only a small group of firms. They *were* drawn from diverse industries, and their behaviour *was* consistent over a period of time in which the external environment changed considerably. Nevertheless, the question might be asked: is there any lasting lesson to be gained from a study of a few dozen companies which may or may not be typical in their management problems? This chapter addresses that question.

Earlier chapters referred to other studies of management, and in Chapter 3, a number of contradictions in our understanding of the impact of management were attributed to the often implicit assumption that all managers act alike, except for idiosyncratic differences (or perhaps differences in the approach to management in the business school they attended). But management does influence the organization. Any systematic differences between the managements of different organizations, therefore, are important for understanding their organizations.

I have suggested that a balanced management type may be the ideal, but it is not the only alternative to the clear sub-system dominance we found in the three industries studied. This chapter develops the logic of the model in its expectations about the behaviour of other management configurations. It goes on to explore systematically (but not statistically) the behaviour, and success or failure, of a larger number of firms and industries by considering the extent to which a sub-system dominance or bias has affected their actions.[1]

MANAGEMENT TYPE AND THE TASK ENVIRONMENT

Throughout this book, I have treated organizations as consisting of three basic sub-systems. In Chapters 1 and 2 the three sub-systems of the organization were outlined. The technical sub-system is concerned with the actual technological function of the organization; the institutional sub-system is concerned with boundary scanning and legitimizing the role of the organization; and the managerial sub-system is concerned with the co-ordination between, and control of, the other two.

Other authors have analysed organizations as consisting of a greater number of groupings (Katz and Kahn 1979; Mintzberg 1983; Williamson 1970). When the numbers are expanded beyond the three basic groupings, however, they cease to have universal relevance for all organizations and become specific to the type of organization. If one distinguishes between production and production maintenance in manufacturing firms, for example, there is no obvious analogy when dealing with service firms, particularly those which are in the public sector. Production maintenance either ceases to exist or becomes part of the organizational development function. When only the three categories are used – what the organization does, control and co-ordination of these activities, and legitimization – it is possible to consider relatively pure cases in which one form of dominance develops, and to consider the type of behaviour which results.

Who's in what sub-system

It may help if we begin by relating these three sub-systems to the common functions carried out within a business organization. The technical sub-system of a financial institution is made up of those people who manage the borrowing from depositors and the lending and investing of money. The managerial sub-system includes those people concerned with human resources, resource allocation, internal auditing and control systems, and the co-ordination – *but not the implementation* – of the deposit and lending policies of the organization. The institutional sub-system would be concerned with broader issues of boundary scanning and legitimation, including forecasting future economic trends, government and industry liaison, lobbying, and public relations.

Within construction firms, the technical sub-system consists of those people who construct houses or develop property; the institutional sub-system consists of the sales and marketing staffs, and those involved with governmental and inter-organizational liaison; and the managerial sub-system includes the accounting, personnel, and legal specialists.

Within a manufacturing firm, the technical sub-system includes the production and product research and development sections; the institutional sub-system is made up of marketing, market research, and public affairs, which could include consumer or customer relations, public relations, stockholder relations, lobbying, or other forms of what economists refer to as 'rent-seeking'. Finally, managerial functions again include resource allocation and control, including human resources, inventory control, and finance.[2] It is worth noting that despite the commonly expressed management cliché, 'human resources are our most valuable resource', none of the firms within the smaller longitudinal sample and only one in the broader range of firms to be examined in this chapter, had senior managers whose background was in human resources (or personnel) management.

Within each organization, therefore, all jobs or sections can be classified as being in one or more sub-systems. But the classifications might be different for different firms. For example, while marketing can always be considered part of the institutional sub-system, product sales in some firms could be considered a part of the technical sub-system. This would be the case in organizations which are essentially sales organizations – they either do not produce the product themselves, or production is only a minor part of their activities. This would be likely to be the situation in firms with a simple technology and relatively low production costs.

In setting out this typology, individuals and positions have been considered interchangeably. A position is within a certain sub-system and the individual holding the position falls within that sub-system as a result of having either experience or educational qualifications which fit the needs of the position. But there are divergences from these tidy pigeonholes. These divergences can relate both to the individuals themselves and to the positions they are expected to fill. They produce a hybrid type of manager which allows us to consider more than the pure types we have dealt with to this point.

Classifying managers within the smaller sample was relatively straight-forward. The typical technical banker had spent his life within banking, most commonly having once been a teller.[3] Similarly, the typical technical developer started as a small housebuilder and became a senior manager of a larger firm through either growth or merger. The administrative managers also tended to have clearly defined backgrounds and career paths which made the assumption of bias quite reasonable. When we move to the more diverse grouping of firms, the number of mixed-types or hybrids increases. But the recognition of mixed types also allows us to describe firms in more diverse ways and, as we will see in Chapter 7, this becomes more important when we consider the design of organizations.

In the first place, there may be a mixture of educational backgrounds. For example, an engineer with an MBA who had worked in each of the production and managerial and institutional functions could be considered to span all of the sub-systems. Similarly, someone with an education which emphasized one sub-system but job experience in another could produce a balanced manager, or at least one with a mixed bias. This would depend to a large extent upon the form the experience took. Of the two most senior managers in one of the construction firms studied, one was trained as an accountant, the other as a lawyer. Neither had any experience in the industry when they joined the firm. The lawyer took an interest in the technical aspects of the industry, and spent a great deal of time learning about it. By the time he had been with the firm for five years, although his legal training might have still been producing some form of vocational bias in the lawyer's decision processes, it could no longer be considered to be an administrative/control bias. The accountant, on the other hand, took little interest in the day-to-day production of the firm, but he did spend a considerable amount of time dealing with the 'industry' as a whole. The result was a balanced management type as the two men between them represented all of the three sub-systems. This is also one of the two Canadian construction firms which emerged from the 1982 recession intact and are still in the construction business, albeit vastly altered.

Another type of hybrid is the individual whose position is expected to span two sub-systems. A classic example of this type in the literature has always been the research manager who is expected to perform both managerial and technical functions. In the public sector, this type of hybrid is exemplified by the street-level bureaucrat – the technical expert in service delivery is also the major representative of the organization to its task environment and, therefore, a major factor in legitimation.

The most common case of individuals expected to represent more than one sub-system are senior managers themselves. They are required to act to legitimize the organization, performing what Pfeffer and Salancik (1978: 16) consider to be their symbolic role; they are expected to co-ordinate and control the activities of the entire organization; and they are expected to ensure that the technical functions are performed and the core is protected.

But senior management may not have the experience, training or perspective to meet these expectations. The confusion between managerial functions and management can lead to a circumstance in which only the managerial sub-system is represented within management. This in turn can produce a senior managerial group preoccupied with control and out of touch with the environment and technology of the organization and the problems faced within each. That is not to say that the managerial functions of co-ordination and control are not the responsibility of those in control, but they can be carried out by others. These managerial functions are what Urwick (1937) considered to be the 'staff' functions and are commonly carried out by individuals and units not in the direct operational structure of the organization.[4] Those carrying out these functions are buffered or isolated from the rest of the organization and neither interact with the environment, nor relate to the core technology of the organization. Not, perhaps, the best prescription for the role of a senior executive.

The role of management

Thompson developed three hypotheses with respect to the composition of what he referred to as the 'inner group' of the organization, which others have called the dominant coalition, and we have considered more directly as the upper echelons or senior management of the organization. The *first* was that in a turbulent and uncertain environment, institutional specialists would be represented within management. The *second* was that in organizations with an imperfect or complex technology, the technical sub-system would be represented. The *third* was that in organizations which were large, and had a diversity of tasks or conflicting goals, the managerial sub-system would be represented. In essence, the control of the organization would rest with those who understood the critical contingencies which the organization might be expected to face, at various points in time.

Thompson's hypotheses indicate, under 'norms of rationality', that those in control will be most likely to be those best able to solve the *last* problem the organization faced. Yet the zig-zag nature of the decision-making process with a built in lag before problems are recognized, a further lag to enlarge the search area, coupled with its cyclical attention to problem resolution, makes it almost certain that today's problem will not be at all the same as yesterday's (Greiner 1972). It is the unintended consequences and the reshaping of the organizational equilibrium resulting from resolving one problem that produces the next problem or opportunity. I suggested in the last chapter that handling the critical contingencies the organization faces requires a balanced management type. But if a balanced management type is not possible, at the very least, those in control of the organization should be knowledgeable of what it is the organization does and, to a lesser degree they need to be aware of the environment in which the organization functions.

The argument for balance made in the last chapter follows from a different logic than that of the 'norms of rationality' of rational models (Thompson 1967). Such models do recognize that organizations require different management types at different points in time in order to respond to the fluctuating needs of the environment and the organization. They assume, however, an ability to recognize what is desirable and to bring about that change. In the absence of this condition it would appear to be better to assume that anything can happen and, like Lord Baden-Powell, 'Be Prepared'.

If there is a lack of representation or bias at the top, this will also tend to be reflected and exaggerated in the rest of the organization (Carroll 1990c). The traits of the leaders tend to filter throughout the organization (Downs 1967) and, as decision-making moves downward in the organization, interaction remains within the same sub-systems as those represented by the top management (Jenkins 1978). It cannot be assumed that, if the senior management are unconcerned with marketing or quality control, the rest of the organization will be, any more than it can be assumed that once someone unconcerned with marketing and cost control reaches the top of the organization these will suddenly become their overriding interests.

An example of this latter problem is found in the literature on public organizations. The requirements of service and neutrality demand that civil servants should follow rules, and implement them in an objective and impassionate manner (Kernaghan 1984). However, when these same civil servants reach a certain point within the hierarchy they are expected to unlearn this behaviour and begin to use subjective forms of judgement and to take risks. Similarly, we expect our politicians to be statesmen, yet the process of becoming a successful politician requires anything but statesmanlike behaviour. A prescription based upon 'unlearning' may be nice but it is not logical (Starbuck and Nystrom 1988).

The process of managerial succession tends to reward either those like the current management or those best able to solve the problems of the past. There is also the inability on the part of organizations to recognize and respond to environmental change. As a result, neither the management representation dictated by 'norms of rationality', nor balanced representation, is likely to occur naturally. Our emphasis, therefore, must shift to the practicability of other configurations.

SUCCESSFUL VERSUS UNSUCCESSFUL ORGANIZATIONS

This analysis of more than 100 different firms is based upon an examination of material from the trade press, government reports, business magazines, academic journals and personal interviews. (The firms are listed in the Appendix at the end of the book.) An extensive analysis of the backgrounds of each of the individual senior managers and their educational and work experience was not always possible. This is particularly true for the brief analyses which are drawn from a survey of firms featured in *Fortune* magazine. In these cases conclusions frequently are based on information about only one featured senior executive. While limiting the information available about the other management members, this does allow more variations in types of firm to be considered. In the interviews, moreover, managers tended to discuss the attributes of those individuals whom they felt had been a part of their success – this constitutes an appropriate surrogate for the 'dominant coalition'. In the autopsies of failure, the reasons given for problems often gave a clear indication of biased problem recognition.

Coupled with the more detailed analysis in earlier chapters, this information does help us to develop an interesting picture, drawn from a broad

Table 6.1 Management type and performance

Management type	Breakdown by performance (number and %)		Overall (number and %)
	Successful firms	Unsuccessful firms	Total
Administrative/ institutional	2 (3%)	5 (14%)	7 (7%)
Administrative	5 (8%)	23 (66%)	28 (28%)
Administrative/ technical	16 (24%)	— (0%)	16 (16%)
Technical	7 (11%)	4 (11%)	11 (11%)
Technical/ institutional	24 (36%)	3 (9%)	27 (27%)
Balanced	12 (18%)	— (0%)	12 (12%)
Total	66 (100%)	35 (100%)	101 (100%)

range of organizations, of those management configurations which are most successful and, in particular, of those which survive periods of high turbulence. The results of the study of the 101 companies are contained in Table 6.1. Sixty-six were reports of success stories or successful turnarounds.[5] Thirty-five were cases of unsuccessful management or, at least, corporate difficulties. The results are quite striking in terms of the relationship between success and management type. Eighty per cent of the unsuccessful firms appeared to lack technical representation in management, while 89 per cent of the successful companies clearly had technical representation.

Of the sixty-six successful companies, only twelve had a fully balanced managerial configuration, but only seven entirely lacked a technical component within their senior management. The most common configuration was a combination of technical and institutional – in the case of the manufacturing firms this was usually some combination of production and marketing. Five of the successful companies, however, did have a purely administrative configuration. In the case of the unsuccessful firms the picture is reversed. There were no examples of balanced management and all but seven had an apparent administrative bias in their management. Eighty per cent of the unsuccessful firms exhibited a strong administrative bias.

The differences are equally clear if we calculate the failure rates associated with the absence of each of the three sub-systems. Among the thirty-eight firms with no representation from the administrative sub-system, seven – or 18 per cent – were unsuccessful. Of the fifty-five organizations with managements that excluded the institutional sub-system, twenty-seven – or 49 per cent – were unsuccessful. And among the thirty-seven firms that had no representation from the technical sub-system, twenty-eight – or 76 per cent – were unsuccessful. A balanced configuration is the ideal, but the costs of exclusion depend on the sub-system. Technical representation is most vital, institutional representation comes second in importance, and administrative representation is least essential to the organization's success. This is a similar conclusion to that drawn from our smaller sample in Chapter 3. Administrative managers can hold administrative costs down but they do not seem to be able to translate these higher levels of 'efficiency' into sustained levels of performance.

In the successful firms generally either the CEO had a technical background or other senior members of the management team, who were identified as important to the firm's success, had such a background. Some of these, however, may also have been cases of balanced or mixed representation, although only the technical component of the management team was credited with the success. (It may be that there were members of the management team representing other sub-systems who were simply not mentioned.) In others the CEO either had a mixed background with education in more than one area, such as the chemist with an MBA who ran Gentech, or mixed experience, as with PPG in a number of aspects of the organization. Pepsico (the makers of Pepsi-Cola) were typical of this type of development: 'We expect our personnel people to be in the business up to their eyeballs – to know sales, profits and margins' (Dumaine 1989: 84).

Of those which had an administrative or administrative/institutional domination without any apparent technical representation, it could be argued that these management configurations were providing a necessary ingredient to correct previous biases. The change to an administrative bias at the American NBC television network, for example, followed by vigorous cost-cutting, could have been correcting the technical bias of the previous president, Grant Tinker, who had helped the company to a lead in the ratings, but possibly at high administrative and control costs. This was the reason given for management changes at Pillsbury (US) when taken over by Grand Metropolitan (Kirkland 1989). The new CEO, a former financial analyst, intended to reduce excessive overhead through tight managerial control. While cost cutting may be a necessary and successful way of improving profitability, if the cost cutting is limited to only the technical sub-system, it may occur at the expense of product quality, innovation and market share.

The most common cause of management change appears to be as a result of a take-over or in response to a major problem, usually low profitability or loss of market share. After experiencing major problems in public relations and profitability, a new technical manager at Nestlé's cut back and shook up the 'bloated management' structure (Tully 1989). Black and Decker took over General Electric (GE) and 'replaced a complacent manufacturing mentality with an almost manic market-driven way of doing things' (Huey 1989: 89). The new CEO, an MBA without experience in the industry, fired the old managers and brought in young new administrative managers, *but* among these was also an engineer who did have experience within the company. Zimmerman (1991) later studied GE as a case of a successful turnaround. In its study of restructuring, Business International mentioned management change as the impetus for change in fourteen of their twenty-seven cases.

The need for change also can sometimes be recognized and achieved inside the organization. Lee Iaccoca recognized the error of ignoring the technical core, as pointed out earlier, and corrected it by bringing in senior managers from the technical core, most notably William Lutz, whom he credited with 'an instinctive understanding of cars' (Taylor 1988). He reorganized the management at Chrysler to bring it back to a balanced management with senior managers with backgrounds in production and marketing, as well as administration.

In summary, the successful companies covered a broad range of industries from franchised comedy clubs (Yuk Yuks) to heavy equipment manufacturers (Caterpillar). What they had in common was a recognition of the need for technical sub-system representation and balance. 'Our success is totally dependent upon our ability to anticipate what our guests want' (Izzy Sharp, Four Seasons Hotels). 'You can't make too many of the decisions on the executive floor. You have to depend on the people who are close to the market and technology' (Allen F. Jacobson, CEO of 3M). 'We want to see a willingness to work hard, stay within the system, and go for the next rung on the ladder' (Foodlion).[6]

It should be kept in mind that, unlike the earlier sample, this analysis is not longitudinal. The firms were classified as successful or unsuccessful on the basis of their status at one particular point in time. This may explain some of the anomalies of successful administrative bias and unsuccessful technical/institutional bias. Of the firms which did not conform to our expected pattern, a few would have later needed to be reclassified. J.R. Nabisco, at that time headed by Ross Johnson, was classified as a successful company with an administrative/institutional configuration. A year later the firm was in serious trouble and was considered to be an example of very poor management (Burrough and Helyar 1989). Campeau Corporation, which had technical management for most of the period when it was a residential property developer, is one of the five administrative success stories. Two years after its successful take-over of one of the largest retail clothing chains in the United States, however, the company had filed for bankruptcy protection. As of 1992, these were the only cases in which firms categorized as 'successful' later became less than successful.

Turning briefly to the unsuccessful firms, the high proportion which had purely administrative management supports our hypothesis. Where a mixed management was evident in unsuccessful companies, it was usually an administrative/institutional blend. Of the seven unsuccessful cases which had a technical management without any administrative input, two were examples not only of bias but also of severe problems in business ethics – E.F. Hutton in the United States and Principal Trust in Canada. In the latter case, criminal charges were laid following the failure of the firm.[7] Two others were in the aerospace industry. Northrup Aerospace was a case of not being able to deal with the co-ordination and control problems brought on by rapid growth. This is a circumstance we hypothesized would require administrative representation. Canadair (a Canadian aerospace manufacturing company) was a privatized crown corporation. As a result, it may have lacked an institutional component and thus failed in the area of environmental scanning, an institutional function, rather than through a lack of administrative control.

A case of administrative bias can also be seen within Domtar, a Montreal-based company taken over by the Province of Quebec in 1980. It took three years of poor performance before it began to cut administrative positions as part of an overall restructuring (McKenna 1989). Similarly, Bramalea Construction was on the verge of bankruptcy with $510 million of debentures in default, before it proudly announced that it had slashed overhead expenses by $40 million. Expenditures were cut everywhere, 'right down to photocopying and coffee supplies'.

One other type of company worthy of consideration is that taken over by 'corporate raiders', or conglomerates. The conventional wisdom is that a leveraged buy-out (LBO) will spell long-term doom for most companies as 'preserving a company's soul isn't their long suit' (Lamont 1988: 44). But this need not be so, either with LBOs or simple take-overs. As we see in our next chapter, conglomerates constitute one of our models for ensuring balanced management within an organization. A perspective based on management type and bias would suggest that the difference between successful and unsuccessful conglomerates lies in the type of management put into place after the take-over.

Certainly, Donald Trump's take-over of Eastern Airlines and its subsequent bankruptcy is a case of a non-technical take-over. Conrad Black, on the other hand, has had mixed success in Canada and the United Kingdom. His management of Dominion (grocery) stores and Massey-Harris (farm

implement manufacturers) in Canada were both cases of classic administrative management, and both cases were initially very successful and
subsequently had financial difficulties. He has been remarkably successful,
on the other hand, with the purchase and management of a transnational
newspaper empire, most notably the British *Daily Telegraph* and the
Jerusalem Post. The difference may be that in addition to his 'managerial'
skills, Black is also experienced and knowledgeable about the newspaper
business – the first case in which he was in an industry in which he had a
technical background.

These examples also highlight the partly spurious relationship between
ownership/entrepreneurship and performance. It is often assumed that
those who start up and build the company owe their success to their
entrepreneurial spirit or to the benefits of ownership. This may be partly
true. But what this type of company also has is an owner who understands
the technical aspects of the organization. Those who started construction
companies were engineers, architects or builders. The same is true in a
larger number of companies – and I would suggest that it is the technical
knowledge of the owner/manager, not the fact of owner/management *per
se*, which is the major factor in the success of these firms.

For example, the Irving companies based in New Brunswick, Canada, are a
family-owned diversified group of companies specializing in telecommuni-
cations, oil and forestry. Each member of the family specializes in one of the
technical areas in which the family is involved. The company has had a very
strong record of successful management and K. C. Irving, the patriarch, is
listed by *Fortune* as one of the world's billionaires (Demont 1989a). On the
other hand, Cabot Corporation, an old Boston investment company, ran into
difficulties in the 1960s when the third generation of family management
graduated with a Harvard MBA and 'set out to regularize the company's
management according to modern principles' (Sherman 1989: 138). Recovery
occurred under a technical manager who was not a family member.

While a change in management type is often a function of a change in
ownership, this is not an essential condition. Nu-West Corporation, one of
the builders in our earlier sample, began to have difficulties when it took
the advice of a team from the Harvard Business School and diversified.
Moving from the residential construction business, which its owner and
senior managers understood, the firm diversified into the oil, gas and
transportation industries. New financial specialists were hired at the senior
levels of management. Although the owner retained control, the number of
changes in senior management represented a change in the management
type. If the economy had remained robust, this strategy could very likely
have been a good move. Unfortunately, it did not. Within two years the firm
was in financial difficulty.[8]

Changing domain, or sphere of activity, but not management type can also create problems. British Gas plc went on an 'acquisition' binge after privatization in 1986. Their problems seem to have been a result of overly technical management and insufficient managerial and institutional talent. 'Typically, chief executive Robert Evans, who started with the company in the mid-1950s, is a mechanical engineer by training. He is far more comfortable with gas compressors and pilot lights than with convertible shares and certificates of deposit.' The company is characterized as 'long on skill, but short on financial savvy' (McMurdy 1990: B3). Nevertheless, most of these complaints followed one 'hamfisted' take-over attempt and were made by financial analysts who were perhaps more interested in the share market than the overall soundness of the company. The technical bias they deplored still produced after-tax profits of $1.2 billion in 1989 on sales of $15 billion – an 8 per cent margin.

The First Chicago Bank provides an interesting example of contrasting behaviour before and after a change in management type. It started with a pure technical bias under a man Martin Meyer (1974) referred to as 'Mr Banker', a person whose philosophy of banking was that of a traditional conservative with a community responsibility. I repeat his credo used earlier: 'We believe it is our obligation to assume a reasonable degree of risk in our lending activities. It would have been unfortunate if the banks had moved precipitously to recoup on loans by forcing the troubled borrower to liquidate assets in distressed markets or forced them into bankruptcy' (Annual Report 1975: 2). Instead, the organization opted to concentrate on tightly controlling non-interest expenses. Four years later, a shake-up began which saw almost a complete overhaul of the management, with many of the newcomers coming from outside the banking community. In 1981 alone, nine department heads were hired in such new areas as corporate planning, communications and administration. The philosophy of this new 'First Team' was 'relationship management'. In 1981 operating expenses were increased to provide for the new staff needed for this new direction. At the same time, a 40 per cent decline in income and earnings was experienced.

The results of this survey of a broad and diverse group of firms indicate that there are clear differences in management between firms, even in the same industry, and that these differences are consistent with differences in the sub-system background of the managers and the degree of sub-system representation in the management configuration. Further, they also support our expectation that a balanced management type is the best form, but that – failing balance – technical representation should be considered a necessary, albeit not sufficient, condition for success.

Cyert and March (1963) argue that business firms constitute a special case of organizations which operate in large part in isolation from their social environment. While this may not be as important a distinction today as it was thirty years ago, let us turn to cases in which environmental interaction would be more essential – those of public agencies and highly regulated industries which have a greater reliance upon the institutional sub-system.

VARIATIONS ON A THEME: INDUSTRIES AND PUBLIC ORGANIZATIONS

There is evidence that management type also affects public-sector decision-making. For example, studies have found that the administrative cost levels in public health hospitals and educational institutions are a function of the previous type of experiences of the decision-makers and their perception of themselves as representing the technical or the administrative sub-system (Anderson and Warkov 1961; Grusky 1961; Meyer 1982). Similarly, studies of resource allocation within research organizations and universities have also found that decisions tended to favour the sub-units of the decision-maker (Hall and Mansfield 1971; Pfeffer and Salancik 1974). Thus, the cutting of faculty research budgets rather than administrative costs in university departments can be seen as a result of the deans and department heads having more information about and favouring administrative over technical (research and teaching) concerns.

Similarly, research on higher civil servants in Quebec found that the sub-system representation of senior bureaucrats changed from technical under the Parti Quebecois government of Premier Levesque in the early 1980s, to administrative after the Liberal government of Premier Bourassa took office. Bureaucrats' definitions of their own roles and their priorities for future action were consistent with the difference in the knowledge and experience of the two types of managerial orientations (Johnson and D'aigneault 1988). A similar point arises from Canadian External Affairs Minister Flora MacDonald's (1980) charge that the bureaucracy offered her politically impossible alternatives with insufficient time for analysis. While this might be viewed as either incompetence or a Machiavellian attempt to thwart, it can be more constructively interpreted as the type of problem which emanates from an organization with insufficient institutional representation among its senior officials. Studies of the Department of External Affairs have shown that the importance of the institutional sub-system changed significantly under different leadership, and that it is extremely difficult to maintain an ongoing boundary scanning role when there is little support for this function within the inner group of management (Madar and Stairs 1977; Page 1987).

Studies of the American legal system and of university decision-making suggest that those organizations where the senior decision-making levels were dominated by representatives of the technical and administrative sub-systems were very slow at perceiving and adapting to environmental change – functions which are the responsibility of the unrepresented institutional sub-system (Allen, 1966; Cyert, 1978; Rubin, 1980). Bozeman and Slusher (1979) also found that public organizations dominated by the administrative sub-system were similarly insensitive to the external environment, heaping 'dysfunction upon dysfunction', reinforcing existing areas of search in a form of paralysis which left them unable to produce new technological solutions to the problem. Overall, the literature suggests that the institutional component within public organizations has to be represented in order to achieve effective public control (Gruber 1984), and that under-representation of the technical sub-system can be literally a recipe for disaster – the lesson of the *Challenger* space shuttle disaster (Romzek and Dubnick 1987).

Over-representation of the technical sub-system can be equally problematic. Dunleavy's (1981) study of public housing policy in Great Britain found that due to weak administrative and political control, architects had a disproportionate influence upon public housing policy in Britain in the post-war years. Because of their 'architectural ideology', they defined problems in such a way as to use the technological solutions of their discipline – which was to build large, high-density public housing projects. In his recent research he has also found a systematic difference between government departments in their allocation of administrative costs which is consistent with variations in management type (1989). Meltsner (1976), in his study of policy analysts, also notes how differences in disciplines and training are reflected in differences in the perception of problems and styles of analysis, a finding consistent with French's (1980) research in Canada. All of these studies provide support for the proposition that public organizations also require a balanced management in which no one sub-system has dominance. This is the management type best able to deal with the critical contingencies which can arise from problems in any of the sub-systems.

There is also some limited evidence that changes in the type of management in public agencies affect policy and budgetary outcomes. The change in the management configuration of the US Postal Service from an institutional bias to one of balanced management led to profitability (Baxter 1988). Phidd's (1988) study of the Canadian Department of Finance has shown how changes in the composition and economic training of senior management preceded changes in the outcomes of the organization – in this case, Canadian fiscal policy.

The effect upon both resource allocation and policy is evident in Canada Mortgage and Housing Corporation (CMHC, the crown corporation responsible for the *National Housing Act*). In 1969 it moved from a purely technical type of management in which all senior managers were long time employees with considerable field experience, to a mixed type in which the technical domination was reduced by an influx of institutional representatives, most of whom were political scientists, although the president was a politically active land developer (Campbell and Szeblowski 1979; Carroll 1986). During this period, housing policy switched from a low-key but effective financial emphasis to highly visible, political intervention.

In 1974 the organization underwent another change of management from the mixed type to a purely administrative domination. The proportion of staff devoted to control and co-ordination increased from 15 per cent in that year to 17 per cent two years later and to 24 per cent by 1981. Similarly, head office employees increased from 27 per cent to 34 per cent. Within the head office the proportion of staff devoted to administration increased from 58 per cent to 70 per cent (Carroll 1986). In effect, in an organization with decentralized programme delivery, the number of staff in the field decreased while the number of central staff increased during a period in which the total staff of the organization increased and the total activity of the organization declined. In 1986, CMHC moved to a balanced configuration and, in 1988, was lauded by the Auditor-General of Canada as one of the most efficient, and effective, organizations within the Canadian federal government (Canada 1988). In 1990, it returned to a technical dominance.

When controlled by administrative managers – most notably under President Ray Hession, a former IBM employee – CMHC withdrew from the regulation and control of the housing market, an area it had dominated since 1945 (Carroll 1990b). By 1992, it appeared that the organization would be disbanded as the federal government gave the provinces jurisdiction over housing in a new constitutional agreement. The loss of institutional representation and input is highlighted by the fact that the senior management of the organization apparently found out about the change in constitutional power by reading about it in the newspaper. It would appear, then, that different sub-system representation also affects the perceptions and outcomes of public organizations.

It was noted earlier that in highly regulated industries we would expect to see a need for institutional representation similar to that in public organizations. Deposit-taking institutions and banks are an example of heavily regulated firms in most countries (Lermer 1978; Spellman 1982). They are controlled in terms of ownership, portfolio mix, types of investments and activities and, in some areas, charges and interest rates.

We noted in the last chapter that a lack of technical representation was the cause of failure in a number of Canadian banks and loan companies. A lack of technical representation may also be a part of the problem with the savings and loan industry in the United States. The problem may be not only one of bad lending practices, but also of a management type without

sufficient technical knowledge to be conversant with good lending practices. Certainly, the savings and loan companies which had technical
management in the smaller sample analysed in earlier chapters have fared
better than those with administrative management.

But the industry did not lack institutional representation. In the United
States, the savings and loans industry was bailed out, at great cost and with
only marginal recriminations to those who were responsible for the losses.
This is not to say that there have not been some legal proceedings, and at
least some criminal proceedings, but it appears that the high level of
'rent-seeking' pursued by the industry in lobbying Congress was effective.

On the other hand, the banking industry in Canada demonstrates the cost of
ignoring the institutional sub-system. For years the banks enjoyed a position of
particular coziness in their relationship with government, even being able to
boast that 'they [the banks] wrote the Bank Act'. Yet, in the late 1980s, the
banks found themselves the butt of regulatory action to stop them from
increasing user fees, and on the losing end of an attempt to keep foreign banks
and trust companies from competing with them. They had been acting 'as if'
their environment was benign and favourable, so they did not monitor it nor
respond to it. They were wrong. This may be why there were subsequent
changes to the structure and staff of the Canadian Bankers Association, their
main lobbying group, and it may explain the hiring of former civil servants at
a senior management level by two of the five largest banks.

A similar situation faced the insurance industry in Ontario (Atkinson and
Nigol 1988). The industry had become complacent, believing that because they
provided an essential service, their role was secure. In the areas of automobile
and liability coverage, they pushed prices up and reduced service, assuming no
action would be taken against them. In fact, they ignored two important aspects
of their environment: first, a change in government at the provincial level to the
Liberal party, which was not as sympathetic to big business as its Conservative
predecessor had been; and second, the rising public outrage. They acted as if
they were operating in a controlled, non- volatile environment, and they were
wrong. No effort was made at public relations or lobbying – until they found
their prices regulated.[9]

We can conclude, therefore, that management does make a difference in
terms of the actions or activities of organizations, and also in their success.
Furthermore, this is true for a wide range of private-sector firms in a variety
of industries, and also for organization in the public sector.

CONCLUSION

In this chapter we have moved beyond the narrow confines of statistical
significance and our small group of firms. The results of looking briefly at

more than a hundred firms, rather than examining thirty-four in great detail, have been very similar. Balanced management is the ideal condition for long term performance and viability. Under-representation of any one sub-system creates problems. Ignorance of the institutional sub-system can lead to problems of legitimation when issues of regulation or customer support arises. It leaves the organization prone to surprise when its environment changes. Under-representation of the administrative sub-system tends to produce an organization which is unco-ordinated and lacks financial controls. Under-representation of the technical sub-system will mean the organization loses touch with what it is that it does.

If balance is impossible, a second-best position is to have the type of management configuration which can best cope with change. While administrative management may be preferable in a favourable environment because the organization is not faced with problems of adaptation, it has an inherent bias towards control and the elimination of excess slack. This may explain the preference for this type of management in North America through much of the post-war era.

In an uncertain or unfavourable environment, however, technical management or strong technical representation is essential to ensure that the production core of the organization is protected. Since by definition uncertainty cannot be predicted, it is necessary to consider forms of organizational design which can withstand environmental uncertainty if (when) it occurs. As we have seen, successful management is likely to include an institutional component – these firms stand a better chance of either recognizing environmental change or of being able to negotiate with the environment in order to manage it.

Most management prescriptions tell managers how to act. I suggest that a more effective prescription is to get the structure right, and the actions will follow. Changing the behaviour of the managers themselves is unlikely to be successful. Changing the management will only be successful if the sub-systems represented are changed. Ideally, all sub-systems should be represented, but this may not produce a stable coalition. To the extent that there is any prescriptive element to this model, it suggests that a necessary, albeit not sufficient, condition for continued corporate viability is that the technical sub-system always be represented within the management group. Peters and Waterman's (1982) study of excellence provides a partial example of this condition. The similarities among the successful organizations that they studied were not just an emphasis upon people – their own main lesson – but that, in most cases, the technical sub-system was also always represented in the management group. Management was knowledgeable about organizational survival and control, but also remained aware of the production aspects of the organization, the technical sub-system.

Having recognized how bias develops and persists, it should be possible to develop means of designing organizations in such a way as to overcome managerial bias. We turn to this topic in the next chapter.

7 Overcoming the bias of management

INTRODUCTION

When an organization continuously functions in a non-threatening or favourable environment, it is possible for organizational bias to persist with the organization functioning at a relatively low level of performance, but with resources and markets always available. Alternatively, if the environment is hostile and the bias of the existing management is inappropriate to these circumstances, the organization is likely to experience very poor levels of performance. Recognizing that symptom – but not the underlying cause of the bias within the organization – sometimes leads to a decision to replace the managers. If, inadvertently, the new management group has a more appropriate bias, performance may improve. If the new managers are of the same type as their predecessors, however, poor performance is likely to persist. In that case the question is whether the organization can survive by suffering through until the environment becomes more favourable, or whether it will wither and die.

More than twenty years ago, Shull, Delbecq and Cumming (1970: 220) developed a prescription for ensuring that organizational decision-making was 'ideal'. They suggested that there should be overlapping responsibilities as no single expert or form of expertise can claim total competence. In order to ensure this, they suggested that executive succession should be based upon a broad search process and 'socio-technical' or technical/managerial/institutional interaction because adequate representation is unlikely if search was limited to 'sub-group' cronies. In effect, they recommended a balanced management.

Based upon our analysis to this point, this prescription seems valid, yet much of the current management literature and the actual behaviour of many firms ignore such reasonable advice. The problem is that this advice assumes a degree of rationality which does not exist. Senior managers or those in control of the organization do not broaden their search and recognize the impact of bias, if the organization is not in serious difficulty. Instead, they base their actions upon that most unhelpful of pop prescriptions 'if it isn't broken, don't fix it'. This chapter is concerned with means of ensuring that the organization will not break – a lesson perhaps in preventative maintenance and design.

There are means by which organizations can attempt to deal with organizational bias. I outline four of these methods, including the assumptions behind them, and the way in which they might work. In all cases, the basic assumption is one followed throughout this book; it is unlikely that the organization will be able to change the basic behaviour of its managers. If you cannot change the person you must change the personnel. Alternatively, you can change the structure of the organization so as to force changes in the organization's actions. That is, you can structure the organization so the managerial bias of individuals acts in a positive rather than negative way for the organization.

It is probably self-evident that any prescription for preventative maintenance and design to counter the effects of organizational bias must rest upon active, informed self-conscious human interaction. It is the organizational equivalent of Adam Smith's 'invisible hand' that creates the problem, and bias is a serious problem precisely because it is not automatically self-correcting. There must be someone – an owner, a board of directors, or the senior managers themselves – who recognizes the existence of bias, sees it as a problem, and is prepared to act in unfamiliar and uncomfortable ways to correct it. They must be ready and able to act directly to alter the composition of the management group in an appropriate way, or to act indirectly to structure the organization so that it will produce an appropriate range of backgrounds within its senior ranks. The four methods for dealing with organizational bias outlined in this chapter are only limited or partial solutions, but they are workable and reasonably effective. As we shall see, the shoal upon which they most frequently founder is this very need for active, informed and self-conscious interaction at the top.

'NORMS OF RATIONALITY'

The first way to deal with bias is to do nothing, waiting instead for the organization to conform to *norms of rationality*. In this case the organization consciously tries to adapt to environmental change, and to its potential symptom of poor performance, by rational action. It can strive to conform to these norms of rationality by replacing the existing management and management type with managers of a different type who are better able to deal with the current problem. The 'new' management can force adaptation by changing the structure of the organization, or by seeking to change its environment. But, as I pointed out in Chapter 1, this is unlikely to occur unless:

1   the organization is controlled by some external owner or agency which does not share the bias of the organization itself, and which is able to identify the perceived source of the problem and take action; or
2   the organization is in such a state of crisis that any action taken has to be different, dramatic and likely to succeed; or
3   the organization is fortunate enough to have omniscient and altruistic management.

And these circumstances do occur. A combination of 1 and 3 seemed to have been at work with one of the firms in the sample – Cadillac-Fairview Corporation – and this appears to have been the outcome of a pattern of rational strategic planning and decision-making. The Corporation was formed in 1974 in a merger of two construction companies. Until 1980 much of power and decision-making within the company was held by Yves Diamond, long considered one of the most respected developers in Canada (Goldenberg 1981). In 1980, at the beginning of a period of economic recession, a new president took over. He was an accountant and the former president of the holding company trust which owned a large share of Cadillac-Fairview. His appointment was accompanied by change in a number of other senior management positions. The following year the company went out of the residential construction business entirely, closing down its construction arm and selling out its apartment portfolio.

The change in management evolved, one has to presume, from the owners (or the management) themselves. But there was a change in management closely followed by a change in the domain of the organization from residential development to finance. If the change in domain had not taken place this might have developed into an example of a change in management type from technical to administrative, but because the change in domain was to an area of finance – the field of expertise of the new management – new and different technical requirements were matched by new technical skills.

A competitor of Cadillac-Fairview made a similar change in domain at about the same time, but with less successful results. Campeau Corporation, headed by Robert Campeau, also moved out of the residential construction and real estate management business with coincidental changes in the management of the organization, but not in the management type. Campeau Corporation stayed in real estate, emphasizing shopping centres, and eventually moved into the ownership of retail department stores (Gibbins 1989). Unfortunately, neither change in domain was accompanied by the development of a new technical capability. While management changes took place, they resulted in new management – not a renewed technical management. The previous technical management representation, typified by Campeau's own experience in residential real estate, remained. This was an appropriate management type for the real estate industry, but not for a quite different industry where it acted as a maladaptive form of management. This may have been particularly unfortunate because the bias of technical management in the real estate industry in Canada tends to be towards risk-taking. When entering a new domain without experienced management, the risk aversion of Canadian administrative managers might have been preferable. Within a short period of time the firm was in financial difficulty. Bailed out by yet another large Canadian property developer, Olympia and York Developments, a change in management type then occurred. The new management was solidly administrative with an interest in financial control, as would be expected by management put into place by the company's bankers. The retail stores were sold off, thus eliminating the need to develop a technical capability in that area (Philip 1989). The company continues to operate in a scaled down version as Camdev, without Campeau.

Both of these cases are examples of organizations conforming to 'norms of rationality'. In the case of Cadillac-Fairview the impetus to act rationally came from within the organization, while for Campeau Corporation rational norms were externally imposed following a crisis. I am not suggesting that all of the problems of Campeau Corporation were a function of management type, but it does seem that the absence of an appropriate or balanced management configuration and, in particular, the movement into a new domain when lacking technical expertise, may have been a major contributor to the lack of recognition of the seriousness of the organization's problems until a crisis occurred.

Another case of imposed change which fits our definition of rationality occurred in an almost classic example of coalition reformulation. A small manufacturing firm called Enfield enjoyed considerable success in the Canadian market. Its founder and President (but not majority owner), Peter Blair, had been lauded in the press for being an excellent manager, an example of someone who knew the business well but also had hired good administrators as part of the management team. In the classification used in this book the company was a mixed technical/administrative management type. What was ignored, however, was the position of the minority shareholders, and one very large minority shareholder in particular – the Bronfman family. This ignoring of the institutional sub-system or being unaware of problems in the environment led to a high level of dissatisfaction on the part of the Bronfmans. In a messy boardroom battle fought out on the front pages of the newspapers and subsequently in the courts, Blair lost control of his company, losing both his position as president and his seat on the board of directors.[1] Ignoring the needs of a portion of the task environment and assuming they were an acquiescent or passive part of the organizational coalition resulted in the restructuring of the organizational coalition with the previously ignored sub-system now in control (Noble 1989a, 1989b).

A case of internal change occurred within one of the financial institutions. In 1972, Bankers Trust was an established, full service, New York-based multi-bank holding company. It had 200 branches throughout the New York area and in subsidiaries throughout the state. In 1975, however, faced with poor performance, a new president with a background in corporate finance rather than retail banking was hired. Corporate finance had traditionally been an area in which the firm had been weakest. This move to bolster management within an area which had been traditionally weak, or to compensate for a previous bias, had interesting results. By 1981 the firm had closed many of its branches and sold its credit card division. Finally, in 1983, it announced a decision virtually to eliminate traditional banking activities and move almost exclusively into corporate finance (Hector 1984). It should be noted that the period between 1975 and 1978 was marked by almost a complete change-over in the senior staff of the company. It had exchanged one form of bias for another, or one form of technical bias for another. It was similar to the Cadillac-Fairview example as the change in management type preceded the change in domain.

This form of change is likely to occur in cases where there is an owner or external agency who can recognize the perceived problems of the organization and can impose a change or, alternatively, in those rare cases of gifted management which is either implicitly or explicitly rational. It is also more common in cases where there is not a critical time constraint placed upon the organization, giving the management time to consider rather than simply responding to a crisis. Frequently change occurs, or is imposed, as in the case of Campeau Corporation, when the company is on the verge of collapse – in part because the bias of management meant a problem was not recognized as such until it became critical. There are few examples of rational change in management type which is successful at saving an unsuccessful firm – I could find none but am prepared to accept that such cases may exist. The firm or its bankers usually wait too long before forcing adaptation upon the organization so that the 'vicious circle' referred to in Chapter 3 is too far along to halt.

The clarion calls each decade or so for a 'new' kind of manager – from managers to leaders to entrepreneurs and back again (Czarnlawska-Joerges and Wolff 1991) – to practise different types of management practices, in a different organizational structure, comes close to a form of lagged 'norms of rationality'. Having waited until it was clear that the environment has irrevocably changed as noted by all the business magazines and newspapers, organizations take steps to adapt latterly to fit it. 'Lean and mean' of the late 1980s which slashed staffs has given way to 'niche marketing' and 'short run' production in manufacturing. This has meant in manufacturing firms which have successfully adapted, not only a change in structure, but a substantive change in technology from the 'long batch' production identified by several authors (Woodward 1969; Feschuk 1992; Gibbons 1992).

As norms of rationality are uncommon or take too long to come into effect, it is necessary to consider means by which the organization can be designed either to reduce the impact of bias when it does exist or to accommodate it without the need for brilliance, luck or a crisis.

'STRUCTURED BALANCE'

The next two methods involve structuring the organization to avoid or minimize bias. The first of these, *structured balance*, is intended to prevent bias from developing. In this case the organization itself, or the method of managerial succession within it, is highly structured to ensure that there is a continual balance of management types.

It assumes that the power of individuals within the management group will be roughly equal. It requires that managers can recognize the difference between problems which affect the viability of the organization and those that do not; and that having made this distinction, inappropriate managers will voluntarily cede power to another, more knowledgeable group. Thus, when a problem requires that one or two members within the management group be given temporary ascendancy, the other members must be willing to cede power, and later the group which attained power must also voluntarily give it up. These circumstances necessary for balanced structure to exist are exactly the three conditions which we outlined in Chapter 1 as being unlikely to occur in organizations. It constitutes a form of federalism in management and also tends to have many of the problems of federal states.

Structured balance is similar to the type of gifted management which is able to view all parts of the organization, and which Barnard suggested would occur rarely, if ever. Of the 135 firms in the two samples of this study, the clearest, most consistent case of balanced management was the Brascan conglomerate. The firm is owned by two Bronfman brothers and has interests in construction, financial institutions and merchant banking, and mining, amongst others (Best and Shortell 1988). Upon take-over, the original management team within each of the very diversified sets of companies were usually left in charge of their organization and allowed a high degree of decentralized control. For example, despite the change in ownership of Noranda (a large mining firm) many of the employees may not have been aware of the change. Alfred Powis, the president, who led a strong technical representation among the senior managers, remained in control of the company.[2] In each of the firms there is a strong technical management whose knowledge and respect within their own industry is high. At the same time, there is a group of 'controllers' within the head offices of the conglomerate itself. They set overall standards for all of the firms, but they do not become involved in day-to-day decision-making. The institutional representation is maintained through the owners who provide a 'culture' within which all of the firms work and which is communicated to the larger business environment.

A similar pattern is found in Hanson Trust, a British-based diversified transnational conglomerate whose best-known product may be Lea and Perrins Worcestershire Sauce. Its structure is very similar to Brascan, with a centre level concerned with the managerial and institutional functions.

> Very few individuals at center level have come from a business held by Hanson Trust. This allows the center to make decisions regarding each business without influence of an emotional bias. It also ensures minimal interference in each business, since the executives at the center do not know the details as intimately as those who run the businesses.
>
> (Business International 1987: 54)

It may be that these companies are fortunate in having that combination of gifted management. But the structural lessons could be transferred *if* the owners of other firms are prepared to leave decision-making up to their designates (a situation which requires closely controlled ownership); *if* the managers of the corporate control organization are prepared to leave decision-making to the managers of each of the subsidiaries or divisions; *if* there is an incentive for the self-interest of the managers to coincide with the self-interest of the owners; *if* the owners are fortunate or skilled at finding a group of different managerial types who can work together; and *if* the self-interest of the technical managers coincides with the self-interest of the control managers and the owners.

This is not impossible to achieve, and it is clear that just as there are means of designing regulations within the public sector which provide an incentive for compliance, there are means of designing organizational incentives in which the self-interest of the management is not incompatible with the interests of owners. The last requirement of coincidental 'self-interest' of control managers and shareholders could to some extent be met by encouraging or requiring managers to own shares in the company. The desire for long-term growth, sometimes at the expense of the short-term profits, could also be achieved by giving managers long-term management contracts which specify performance goals over a longer period.

The major advantage of balanced management is that it allows management to 'see all' of its environment. Unfortunately, it also assumes that having seen the environment, it will be possible to correctly identify a problem and respond to it. This means, as in the case of Brascan or Holton Trust, that communications between all of the sub-systems must be sufficiently open that a problem is perceived and discussed before it is defined. If the structure is such that all aspects of the problem can be considered in its definitional state, the chances of bias developing is lessened. Finally, it assumes the power of each of the groups to be equal and that each will concede control to the other in the best interests of the organization.

This last may be the most difficult assumption to meet in reality. Power tends to be one of those 'hygiene' factors (Herzberg 1968) which become most important once they are in danger of being lost. Only in the case of discontinuous task forces can one think of cases in which members of the organization might voluntarily concede power, and only if returning to their original position would not represent a reduction in the power of the individual members.

Another means of organizing power is to have the sub-systems somewhat hierarchically arranged. In the case of Brascan, legitimacy was at the top with the owners, control was in the holding company, and the technical components were at the bottom in the separate divisions or firms. Because of the degree of autonomy, however, the relationship between the control and technical components can more easily be seen as the relationship between line and staff rather than hierarchical linking. The authority of the staff or the holding company came through the owners rather than being direct.

The problem of the young staff member tail wagging the old line member dog, however, is as old as organizations. It may be impossible to maintain such a balance because it requires recognition that proximity to the head is not better, just different. In one interview, a staff-level manager explained with an earnest straight face 'that the level of understanding of field people declines the farther away they are from the head office'. This has proved to be a particular problem with transnationals, which in their attempt to streamline, often close decentralized operations, losing specialized cultural knowledge. 'They (field staff) know that nobody at corporate (headquarters) really understands their problems' (Business International 1987: 74).

This form of organizational design seems to be most effective with large organizations, particularly those which are highly diversified and which have distinct differences in technology amongst the various groups. Thus, the pattern of balanced structure is more likely to occur in large diversified conglomerates.[3] Even when it is achieved, structured balance leads to adaptation problems of its own. The most notable of these is that this form of balanced decision-making requires that each group or representative have input into problem definition and problem solving, and it is implicit that decision-making would be on the basis of consensus. This is time-consuming and on occasion might be almost impossible to achieve. It is also likely that competition for power would not cease to exist, but would simply move farther down into the organization within each of the sub-systems. Thus, there would be a competition within each sub-system, or component of it, to have the power to be the management representative of the sub-system. Both of these problems could be overcome by the existence of a tie-breaker and arbitrator – usually in the form of a chief executive officer or someone at the top of the organizational hierarchy. But, in a circular fashion, that person's ability to make this type of decision would provide him or her with greater power. Their superordinate position could result in an unbalancing of the structure, and the development of bias.

STRUCTURED CHANGE

The third possibility is, *structured change*. A popular British comedy series, 'The Fall and Rise of Reginald Perrin', utilized this form of organizational change. The anti-hero, Mr Perrin, in an attempt to force his booming multinational company into bankruptcy, hired, as the four most senior managers, people who by background and qualifications could not have been less appropriate for their positions. To his, but not to our, chagrin all of them were outstandingly successful in their new positions. In its more realistic manifestation, this form of change is similar to 'sunset laws' in the public sector. Rather than attempting to eliminate the development of bias, it simply tries to prevent it from persisting. It requires regular change in the management, forcing a new perspective upon the organization – as Mr Perrin did – by continually putting a round peg in a square hole.

One of the successful firms within the sample used this method. The president and the chairman of the company, one from the technical and the other from the managerial sub-system, each held their position for only two years and then rotated the position. They were also able to overcome the problems of systemic bias as the head office of the company was also rotated between Canada and the United States. In addition to these two positions, other senior positions within the organization were also regularly rotated.

Structured change can be implemented in two ways. The first is simply by the regular rotation of managerial positions, and by limiting the tenure of individuals within each position. This is the method used by Toyota, American Telephone and Telegraph Co., and McDonnell Douglas Corp. It has also been introduced in the Canadian public service as a means of dealing with the plateauing of middle managers. The second is to fill vacant management positions when they occur with people from a different sub-system from that of the previous incumbent. In both cases, it is assumed that bias will exist. But when new members enter the management group they will bring with them a different bias which will tend to temper the biases of the past. Over time, each management type will at some point or another be in control of the organization, and there will be periods of balance during the various transitions. The impact of the changes will be analogous to the Law of Large Numbers in statistics, where the errors or biases cancel each other out. This is what Downs (1967) assumed would happen with self-interest bias.

The first method is one frequently followed in North American university departments with the chair serving for a term of from three to five years without renewal. The assumptions of the method are first, that there is a large pool of individuals who can do the job, or that it is relatively simple to do; and second, that your errors or omissions, whatever they might be, will be corrected or cancelled by the commissions of your successor. The latter point could alternatively be viewed as hoping that your successor's errors or omissions will be sufficiently different from yours to obviate them. This approach requires that there are large numbers of substitutable positions within the organization which can be rotated.

The problems of this method lie in its assumptions. It assumes that there is no inherent consistent bias within the cadre of people being rotated; and that the responsibilities of the position are easy to take on and conversely to take off. Transferring Canadian External Affairs officers between the technical core (embassies and consular offices) and the administrative sub-system (under-secretary) would be a good example of balanced change. Transferring all of the senior levels of the federal public service among a group of administrative managers is not, for there is a strong administrative bias within the cadre. This is what occurred in Canada during the 1970s and 1980s, and it has become apparent that this form of rotation has resulted in the loss of considerable technical expertise (Carroll 1991).

A variant of this mechanism has, however, worked very successfully at the senior levels in the US bureaucracy, producing balanced management in departments over a long period of time. Although not intended as a means of improving the performance of government organizations, it may have inadvertently achieved this. I am referring to the practice of changing large numbers of senior appointments with a change in the Presidency. Although intended to provide a positive ideological bias acting for the executive, it may have the unintended consequence of preventing other forms of bias from becoming entrenched. This method, however, may be unique to the US government, where the lobbying system and rivalled system (Porter 1978) of private research establishments provide a 'parking space' or alternate employment for those waiting their turns. It also tends to ensure a degree of technical representation at the senior levels, as knowledge of the policy area rather than knowledge of bureaucratic processes often is a major factor in appointments.

This method could work within private-sector organizations where there is a large enough pool of relatively similar functions at a hierarchically equal level so that rotation is possible. For example, in large multinationals there may be a large group of similar divisions with positions of a similar scope and seniority. It could also work if organizations were prepared to pay on the basis of individual experience, rather than position, as is the case with universities. In most organizations it could be implemented by returning to an old system, which used to be common in financial institutions, of rotating managerial candidates through a number of different divisions. It could also work in any set of organizations where there is an ability to 'park' people, perhaps through visiting appointments to universities, secondment to interest-group associations or appointments to 'special' task forces.

This form of structured change could also be adapted to resolve problems of bias within segments of the organization particularly in roles which are boundary-spanning (i.e. those that span more than one sub-system). For example, in an organization with field offices a position required to supervise field offices would not be permanently filled. Instead, managers from the field office would rotate through the position on a fixed-term basis. This would have a number of advantages. In the first place, the incumbent would understand the problems of the field offices. In the second place, they would come to understand the control perspective of the headquarters office. They would undoubtedly receive more co-operation from those they were controlling on the basis of having been in the other person's shoes. Finally, there could be a net saving of staff years if the vacated position was not filled – or filled only on an acting basis. Similarly, any supervisory position could be rotated and shared among willing and capable subordinates – a structured version of 'Queen for a Day'.

A major advantage of this approach is that through rotation there is a strong possibility that balanced managers could be developed; this would provide an almost axiomatic situation of a balanced management type. The disadvantage is that the system can be subverted by the development of a cadre of professional managers who either never developed or have lost their technical knowledge, as happened in the Canadian federal public service (Carroll 1991).

The second means of implementing structured change would not limit tenure within a position, but rather would limit succession. This would work rather like an inverse job description. No matter who is going to succeed the incumbent, it must be someone who is unlike him or her in every important characteristic. If the job was previously filled by an accountant, for example, it now will be filled by a non-accountant. If the previous incumbent was from sales, the position will now be filled by someone from production. In this way, three incumbents through any senior management position would represent balance, and representation from each sub-system would be guaranteed over time. This was the type of programme implemented when Black and Decker took over the appliance division of General Electric, a change discussed in the last chapter. An underperforming technical management was replaced with an institutional management. It also provides an example of when even a technical bias can be less than effective. This is consistent with our lesson from the last chapter that, while technical representation is a necessary condition for continuing success, it is not a sufficient condition.

A variant on the idea of structured change can also be seen in the work of Starbuck and Nystrom (1988). The prescriptions for 'camping on see-saws' and building organizational tents rather than castles are means of trying to achieve structured flexibility. The apparent inability of organizations to achieve this level of flexibility could be overcome by the introduction of structured change. Structuring of the change would overcome some of the problems of uncertainty avoidance because the change would be known and programmed. It would provide a measure of certainty for the organization.

A major drawback of structured change is related to the desire for uncertainty avoidance. If the structuring of the change becomes too rigid, the advantage of change in enhancing flexibility and acting to counteract bias by changing the direction of management, could be lost. This tendency to routinization is one of the structural characteristics of organizations discussed previously, and is tantamount to establishing rules for using judgement.

Structured change is more amenable to societies like the United States, which have a high tolerance for uncertainty and a low level of power distance; that is, ones that are essentially egalitarian with low levels of deference. Thus, while it might work in the American organizations where changes in management occur regularly and are expected and accepted, it is less likely to operate successfully in Canadian firms where, outside of professional sports, a tradition of firing even unsuccessful managers has never developed.

'STRUCTURED BIAS'

Our fourth and final solution simply accepts that organizations will be biased, and strives only for the best (or 'least worst') match between the systemic bias of the country and the bias of each management type. In the case of Canada, for example, this *structured bias* solution implies technical management. While in some industries or firms there would be a need for some institutional component, we would expect it to be less essential in Canada. The control requirements would be met through systemic uncertainty avoidance, the institutional requirement would be met both through the relatively stronger statist or corporatist traditions in Canada, where the state tends to act to protect the interests of business, and the higher degree of deference which makes such actions as minority stockholder or consumer activism less likely.

In the United States, on the other hand, while technical representation is advisable, managerial or institutional representation may also be desirable to compensate the higher individual risk-taking proclivities of US managers. This is a refinement of the findings of the earlier part of this study which looked only at two management types, and which seemed to suggest that differences in management were more relevant in the United States with administrative managers having higher levels of performance during times of economic growth. As was pointed out in Chapter 5, however, that may have been an aberration of this sample in which administrative managers of savings and loan companies in the United States during the 1970s enjoyed high earnings while pursuing risky strategies. The lesson overall is that on average over time, firms with technical management will earn higher profits. The lesson from the broader sample which looked at the greater range of firms in the 1980s suggests that technical representation is also a desirable condition for success. It now seems likely, however, that the problem of decline in international competitiveness in US businesses has arisen as a result of the decision-making patterns of the administrative form of management (Reich 1987). Thus it may be only in those countries, at early or rapid stages of development, in which little market co-ordination or control exists, that a managerial dominance is appropriate.

A temporal perspective can help to explain why this form of dominance developed in the United States. In order to control organizations in the period of rapid growth following the Second World War, administrative specialists may have been required. But this should be seen as a transition period necessary to bring discipline and control to firms that had expanded quickly. It should not have been viewed as a long term solution.

A response which takes into consideration the systemic needs of country conforms most closely to the need to recognize how managers actually act, rather than how they should act, and it does not place as heavy a burden of rationality on individuals. In essence, it becomes the least worst case solution – bias is accepted as existing and expected to continue, but it is recognized as such and systemic values are used to counteract it rather than reinforce its problems.

The fundamental obstacle to this approach is that the prescription is for a management type *other* than that which is most valued by the culture. Given that those who select senior managers usually share the cultural bias, it will be difficult or impossible to convince most such people to have the appropriate type of managers. It does suggest, however, that multinationals that send in foreign managers and imported management styles which are designed to correct for systemic bias may often succeed in counterbalancing bias in the host country.

This suggestion has implications for other countries as well. If we return briefly to a consideration of Hofstede's 'work-related values' which were discussed in Chapter 4, there are two which have implications in terms of management structures. In countries with a high level of individualism, the administrative sub-system may need more emphasis as a means of controlling the idiosyncratic and entrepreneurial tendencies of the management. In countries which already have high systemic levels of uncertainty avoidance, strong administrative representation which would reinforce these tendencies would be counter-productive. While these hypotheses go far beyond the scope of our original study, they tend to be supported by other cross-national research (Carroll and Joypaul 1992) and are consistent with Hofstede's (1980) own expectations.

CONCLUSION

Each of these methods could work within some organizations. None will work for all. The differences are highlighted when they are compared on the basis of three criteria which are important in evaluating any prescription – workability or effectiveness, acceptability and the ability to achieve long term change within the organization (I will call this stability).

'Norms of rationality' requires some deliberative group – an omniscient owner, a balanced board of directors or a cabinet – who can and will take the time to develop a strategy and then select not only a structure but also the types of senior management required for implementation. This requires both an outside group with power and a form of limited tenure for incumbents. It is very effective when it can be achieved, but it demands an extraordinarily independent and wise guiding hand. Its acceptability is limited to those who will benefit from the changes, and this is not the current management. It can be successful in the long term only so long as the same deliberative group has the knowledge and power to bring about continued change.

'Structured balance' would be the most effective approach *if* it could work. It does not require matching the type of management with an accurate assessment of problems because it has the ability to scan all parts of the task environment. It is the method most commonly prescribed by management consultants and also the method which overlooks individual interests and behaviour the most consistently. It is also, therefore, the means least likely to produce a stable organizational solution because it dismisses the role of power in the organization and the tendency towards structural rigidity. It is also unlikely to be accepted as it assumes that individuals can recognize the merits of knowledge unlike their own.

'Structured change' has most of the advantages of structured balance without the problems of individual psychology. It requires a relatively large talent pool, however, and relative interchangeability of tasks. If improperly implemented, it can also have disastrous results in producing an organization in which uncertainty is so high good performers would be inclined to leave. In addition, there can be a tendency within the organization to develop artificial rigidities to overcome the internal appearance of chaos. The second method of simply changing the type of person at the end of periods of incumbency or tenure would be relatively simple to implement, if it were possible to overcome the tendency to develop rigid classification systems. It would be effective, but demands for uncertainty avoidance would tend to make it both unacceptable and unstable.

This leaves us with the last proposal, which recognizes the existence of bias, recognizes the difficulty of alleviating or eliminating it and suggests that the preferable alternative may be simply to structure the best possible organization given that bias will exist. As it would never achieve either the most appropriate management for the time or an ability to scan all of the task environment, it would be less effective than the other three solutions. It would, however, be stable as it does not require any change and it is not dynamic. It is unlikely, however, that management of organizations would accept this as a reasonable prescription because it requires them to act in a way that is counter-intuitive.

None of these four responses to bias is likely to be entirely effective, and each is appropriate for only particular types of organizations. Nevertheless, together they constitute a workable, potentially effective package which can at least partly counterbalance the effects of bias. The main obstacle is their acceptability to those with the power to shape and change organizations, not their effectiveness once adopted.

On occasion we find people who control organizations acting in ways which suggest that they have at least an intuitive grasp of the central ideas of this book. If those ideas enter the mainstream of our understanding of how organizations work (perhaps in a quite different form that reflects the extensions and refinements offered by other authors) we may eventually find a larger number of organizations that are guided by men and women who recognize the problem of organizational bias and understand the solutions that are available. Nevertheless, even the most optimistic of authors must accept that these proposals are unlikely to easily achieve general acceptance. This book has been guided by the principle that it is futile to demand that managers should behave in ways that are entirely foreign to their experience, values and self-interest. That same principle must shape our understanding of what can reasonably be expected of those who have ultimate authority over organizations – their owners or directors. As the next and final chapter explains, however, there are ways in which the experience, values, self-interest of owners and directors, or managers, themselves may make it possible for them to implement these methods of countering organizational bias.

8 Must bias persist?

The goal of this book has been to expand the scope of models of the decision-process in organizations to encompass important types of non-rational behaviour. We have found that by incorporating the notion of bias into the model, our ability to predict the behaviour of organizations is substantially improved. It is not clear, however, that the diagnosis of 'bias' leads very directly to a remedy. The revised model can tell us why organizations fail to learn and adapt, but its capacity to suggest workable solutions is much more modest. The essence of the problem is that most organizations cannot conform to 'norms of rationality' because to do so requires their managers to act in ways which are inconsistent with patterns of rational individual behaviour – it requires, in effect, that we ask water to flow uphill. Thus, while theories of organization and management may be able to explain, and even predict, failure, they will be less successful at preventing it.

This study has shown that it is possible to classify the management configuration of firms into a series of specific types based upon the background and experience of the senior management. More importantly, it has shown that the decisions, strategies, and outcome preferences of organizations vary systematically across firms and across industries in a fashion consistent with the bias of their management.

The neo-Weberian model outlined and tested in Chapter 1 integrates both behavioural and structural theories of organizational decision-making. It perceives the organization 'as the outcome of a variety of decisions taken by one or more coalitions in the context of bounded rationality and environmental and structural constraints' (Kimberly and Rottman 1987: 17). The structure of the organization in turn is affected by a number of environmental factors of which the most important is the function of the organization. But what this model cannot explain is why organizations do not learn and adapt, and why some then subsequently fail. I have suggested that there are systematic sources of bias within organizations which produce an element of non-rationality which limits the ways in which problems are defined and the choices are made. The two most powerful sources of bias are systemic values and the education and experience of senior managers. When these are added to the model, as was done in Chapters 3 and 4, its ability to predict action is improved. Moreover, as we saw in Chapter 6, the form of managerial bias within organizations can help to explain the difference between those that are successful and those that are not.

The type of behaviour described in this book is not a newly discovered phenomenon, but this analysis has provided a label, 'bias', and a classificatory model of management type which explains a number of actions recognized in the organizational literature (Dutton and Ottensmey 1987; Frederickson 1986; Ford and Baucus 1987). The underlying and previously unrecognized similarity is that these actions reflect the fact that the decision-making process of the organization has functioned in a non-rational manner, thus giving the impression of organizations behaving in unique, unpredictable ways. When this behaviour is considered to be the result of a specific 'bias', a predictable pattern can be detected. The addition of bias to the model provides an explanation for many observations of organizational decline in which no action was taken, or inappropriate were chosen, with correction not being achieved until a point of crisis (Weitzel and Jonsson 1989).

I would hope that most readers of the book have been able to identify with some of the organizations and some of the problems discussed. Certainly, the suggestion that someone within the senior management should be from the technical sub-system and, therefore, knowledgeable about what business the organization is in, should strike a resonant chord. The reader is asked to take a simple test. Look at any organization which has persisted for more than thirty years and see if it is not the case that there has been consistent technical representation at its senior management level.

The question remains, if bias can be recognized and corrected, why does it persist? Prescriptions for overcoming bias can be developed, but they are likely to have only limited success for many of the same reasons that other prescriptive solutions to organizational problems have failed. These reasons include the 'nickel and dime' effect of decision-making; structural rigidity within the organization; and the lack of any outside agency which can replace the management. Bias persists because of the nature of the decision-making process itself and the role of management – managers control the decision-making process and are provided by the structure with the information they want and request, not the information they need but do not request. As a result, managers tend to work with 'myths', to act as if certainty exists when it does not, and to perceive problems as caused by factors other than themselves (Harrison *et al.* 1988; Millikin 1987). This brings us back to the questions raised in Chapter 1. Who replaces the managers? Will rational managers admit that they cannot do their jobs? If bias exists throughout the organization, or in the most powerful echelon, who will recognize it? Who recognizes that the emperor has no clothes, and who tells him? As I pointed out in Chapter 1, it is unlikely to be the consultant whom the existing managers hired and are going to pay.

Hage, in answering the question of whether leadership makes a difference, concluded:

> Yes – provided the set of leaders recognizes the *need for balance* in priorities over time and *correctly* identifies current organizational deficiencies and then chooses the *appropriate* actions to correct these deficiencies.
>
> (Hage 1980: 158) [emphasis added]

But, as with teaching management skills, his emphasis is upon the process involved. The correctness and appropriateness of the actions as seen through whose eyes? Judgement about correctness and appropriateness requires a knowledge of the context of the actions which may be more important than simply learning a process. Similarly, balanced management is unlikely to be achieved without some form of external intervention.

While it was recognized some time ago that as 'groups' goals change, leadership needs change and different forms of leadership are demanded' (Gibb 1954: 889), the literature has remained largely silent upon what form or *type* of leadership is demanded under different environmental conditions, limiting itself to discussions of what managerial or leadership skills are necessary. The literature which does exist seems to find new answers after each recession.[1] As we found in Chapter 6, knowledge of the environment of the organization and its technology or function are more important for success than process skills. To the extent, then, that leadership skills are taught without reference to the type of organizationally specific knowledge which is desirable – that is, which management type the organization should have – the emphasis upon such particular skills may lead to further bias in favour of the managerial sub-system with its emphasis upon such process skills such as co-ordination and control. At the least, then, one would suggest that managerial skills be taught on top of technical skills, or alternatively, that senior managers should be provided with technical training or experience – a circumstance found more frequently in European than in North American firms.

This raises yet another question; who are the senior managers? Presumably many of them like to think they are the 'best and the brightest'. Unfortunately, this is not always true. This is not to say that the senior managers are not usually bright, but the assumption that the best minds, or those who are best able to perceive the problem, are those at the top of the organization, may be one of the myths of management. Those in control of the organization *by definition* are those who successfully solved yesterday's problems and, therefore, they may be the source of today's problems, and frequently will not be the best people to solve them.

Added to the very human reluctance in senior managers to recognize shortcomings in themselves, there is the universal desire for uncertainty avoidance which leads the organizations to continue to routinize and to develop control mechanisms. As controls become more heavy-handed, they reduce the effectiveness of the organization and turn the efficiency of bureaucracy (i.e. organization by expert) into organization by functionaries who are unable to evade the rules of control without penalty. Thus, there is an incentive not to be effective rather than an incentive to be so. This emphasis upon control also leads to the conservative bias within organizations and produces the repetitive, ritualistic actions which make the organization appear divorced from its environment.

Uncertainty avoidance promotes the persistence of bias in another way. Both organizations and the individuals who make up the organization tend to avoid uncertainty by acting in the short term. But, if we are to recognize our biases and correct for them, we must act in a fashion which is to our long term benefit but is not in our short-term self-interest. Long-term benefits, however, are less certain than immediate gains and, besides, what is the long term? Therefore, if left to act on their own, managers, even if they were to recognize their bias, would continue to reinforce it. The very nature of bias suggests that, even if a manager recognizes that an organization is overstaffed, he is unlikely to eliminate his own position.

One means of overcoming this problem is to institute rules which force managers to overcome their self-interest and act for the good of the organization – when appropriate to accept uncertainty, or to recognize that they do not have the best solution to the problem and to cede power to those who do. Within organization theory, this prescription is most familiar as the self-correcting (Landau 1973) or self-evaluating (Wildavsky 1972) organization. The difficulty is that these solutions are again based upon an assumption that people will act in a fashion which is inconsistent with their preferences and their self-interest – an assumption which is more wistful than valid.

By their very nature, rules require enforcement of compliance. This produces echoes of the question in Chapter 1 – who will manage the managers? And when do rules become dysfunctional causing structural rigidity rather than preventing it? The nature of individuals when faced with unpleasant rules is to find a way of circumventing them. Thus we start the familiar process of rules leading to rules; control leading to more control.

In Chapter 7, I developed means by which some organizations may be able to reduce or control the negative results of organizational bias. In each case, the problems of acceptability and stability (not workability) formed a stumbling block to the prescription being put into effect and maintained over the long term.

The problems addressed in this analysis have been addressed by others who have been cited throughout this book. The prescriptions provided and the argument being made, however, are intended to go beyond them in avoiding the problem of putting too heavy a burden of rationality on management in terms of what they should do, compared with what assumptions of self-interest and limited rationality would indicate they are more likely to do.

In essence, bias persists because it is rarely recognized and, when it is, there is no incentive on the part of managers to correct it, and rarely any outside agency with the power to correct it.

Those who can replace the managers are the 'owners' of the organization. In public-sector organizations these are the relevant political ministers. In private-sector organizations they usually are the shareholders acted for by the board of directors, although in some situations the 'owners' are the firm's bankers. But there are impediments to their taking action. They must have information, power, and an incentive to act. It is generally accepted that the board is often the creature of the management (Carroll 1989), and thus has little independent information about the organization. Directors' information comes through management and suffers the same limitations as management's information. Thus, while they nominally have the power to act, in practice they have little recourse. Finally, there is the question of incentive. Frequently, the board's interests are aligned more closely with the interests of management than they are with those of diffuse owners; and to the extent that management plays a role in the selection of the board, the two are likely to exhibit the same bias. Only the firm's bankers are exempt. They have power and an incentive to act, but often will act only when it is too late to save the firm. The demands for coalition reformation discussed in Chapter 1 tend to occur only when the firm is in serious difficulty – in crisis, but not before.

We have suggested that the nature of people is to act 'as if' they have knowledge and certainty even when they do not. This perhaps is not a solvable problem. Even when the problem of bias is recognized, it is not in the interests of the manager to act against his or her short-term interests for the longer-term good of the organization. There may, however, be a way out of the dilemma.

The first possibility is in the changing role of the board of directors. The structure of most publicly incorporated boards tends to approximate our notion of balanced management. Outside members are supposed to represent the shareholders (the institutional sub-system), inside board members are the management and presumably will represent their interests, but other board members often are drawn from related industries or major customers of the organization, thereby representing the technical sub-system. Board members in the past have been relatively passive stakeholders of the organization. Greater involvement in the organization on their part would be largely an act of altruism. But where altruism failed, fear of financial liability may prevail. In part as a consequence of take-overs which have hurt minority shareholders, failures which have not protected employees, or simply changing environmental conditions, board members are increasingly being held responsible for the actions of the management and may increasingly come to act as the 'deliberative' group who are themselves relatively unbiased, or who hold different biases against which they measure the performance of the management.

A second, less coercive and potentially more positive possibility is managerial learning. In the introduction, I pointed out that while I would refer to management as a group, it is made up of single individuals who have the potential for learning and using knowledge. Having recognized the potential for bias, they may act to correct it as a means of serving their self-interest by preserving their jobs. As an illustration, suppose that Berthe is the head of a large manufacturing corporation. As a result of instructions from the board, she has been forced to include within the senior management group a 'product quality' vice-president drawn from the production side of the organization who is near retirement. Despite her reluctance to open up the management group to an 'outsider', after a few weeks she comes to notice that his ideas are good, even though he is an engineer rather than a lawyer, and that he can work with her management team. Upon his retirement, she replaces him with another experienced production engineer. Without any prompting from the board, she also creates a new position of 'consumer relations' vice-president and staffs it with an experienced sales representative. A balanced management configuration has been produced.

The final possibility is to consider circumstances in which the short- and long-term interests of the manager coincide. This would happen if we provided the manager with some stake in the long-term success of the organization. This is what normally separates owners from managers within an organization. It is not differences in their knowledge, with 'professional' managers knowing more about the managerial sub-system, or owners knowing more about the technical sub-system, or, if they are the third or fourth generation of diluted ownership, knowing little about either. Rather, it is that most owners have a long-term stake in the organization. (I say 'most', rather than 'all', to distinguish between owners who do have a stake and those such as the corporate raiders of the late 1980s who viewed the organization as a short-term source of funds.)

In these ways it might be more likely that bias, when recognized, could be overcome. The continuing problem is that bias is by definition unrecognized, there is likely to be a disinclination to recognize that bias exists, or for managers to see themselves as the source of the problem – even when failing to do so costs them a lot. Too often prescriptive solutions ask individuals to act in a fashion other than like themselves; to ignore self-interest because it may be for the long-term benefit of the organization. This tends to become an organizational equivalent of the 'tragedy of the commons' when short-term individual rationality produces long-term corporate collective irrationality.

The argument thus comes full circle. What manager can recognize his own biases? Who will manage the managers or replace them? Which of the 'nickel and dime' decisions of the short term affect the long-term viability of the organization?

My suggestions are quite modest for they do not require changes in the basic human behaviour of those who are in charge of organizations. In any of the three ways which I have just described managers may become more able to recognize the need to counter the effects of bias. When this recognition exists, the possible solutions outlined in Chapter 7 become more viable.

Ideally, we would like to have the gifted management which is able to adjust to changes in its environment and always have the appropriate management type in place. In their absence we can structure the organization to produce balance with all of the sub-systems represented; we can structure the organization to produce regular changes in the management type, not just changes in management; or we can ensure that at the very least the technical sub-systems are always represented within the senior echelons of the organization to ensure that someone always knows 'how to play this game'. This will not provide perfect or even overwhelmingly effective organizations all the time in an environment which is changing, and changing quickly. But the effort will be worthwhile if it can aid managers in understanding why their organization behave as they do, and perhaps also point the way to possibilities for improvement.

Appendix

FIRMS IN SAMPLE I

Banks

Canada	United States
Bank of Montreal	Bankers Trust
Bank of Nova Scotia	Continental Illinois Corp.
Canadian Imperial Bank of Commerce	First Chicago Corporation
	Marine Midland Banks
Royal Bank of Canada	Manufacturers Hanover Corp.
Toronto Dominion Bank	

Loan companies

Canada	United States
Canada Permanent Mortgage Corp.	Fidelity Financial Corp.
Canada Trustco.	First Charter Corp.
Montreal Trustco.	Gibraltar Financial Corp.
National Trustco.	Golden West Financial Corp.
Royal Trustco.	Great Western Financial Corp.
Victoria and Grey Trustco.	Imperial Corporation of America
	First Federal Savings and Loan (Chicago)*

Residential development companies

Canada	United States
Bramalea Ltd.	Cousins Properties Inc.
Cadillac Fairview Corp.	Development Corp. of America

Campeau Corp.
Daon Development Corp.
Nu-West Group Ltd*
Trizec Group

Ryan Homes Inc.
Starret Housing Corp.
U.S. Home Corp.

Notes: N = 34
* = missing some years

FIRMS IN SAMPLE II

ABC
AT&T
AM International
Air Canada
American Airlines
Argus Corp.
Associated British Foods
   (Weston Group)

Bank America
Bank of Montreal
Bankers Trust*
Bechtel
Black and Decker
Bramalea*
Brascan

Canadian Imperial Bank
   of Commerce
CBS
Canada Mortgage and
   Housing Corp.
Canada Trustco.*
Canadian Commercial Bank
Cabot Corp.
Carma Development
Central Capital Corp.
Chase Manhattan
Chevron
Chrysler Corp.
Continental-Illinois Bank*

Deere and Co.

Kelloggs
Kodak
Kraft

John Labatt Ltd

McDonalds
Marriott Hotels
Massey Ferguson

NBC
Nestlé
Noranda
Northland Bank
Northrup Aerospace

Ogilvy's
Olympia and York

PPG
Pacific Lumber
PanAm Airlines
Pepsico
Pillsbury
Principal Trust

RJR – Nabisco
Royal Bank of Canada*
Royal Trustco.*

Seagrams
Sears
Seaway Trust

Dofasco
Dome Petroleum
Dominion Stores
Domtar
Dupont

Eastern Airlines
Eaton's
Enfield Corp.

Falconbridge
Fidelity Trust
Financial Trust
First Chicago*
Foodlion
Four Seasons Hotels

G.M.
Genetech
Genstar
Glenfed Trust
Greymac Trust
Guardian Trust

E. F. Hutton
Herman Miller
Home Depot

I.B.M.
Imasco
(K.C.) Irving Enterprises

Stelco

3M
TWA
Texas Air
Toronto-Dominion Bank*
Trilon

U.S. Air
U.S. Steel
United Airlines
United States Postal Service

Victoria and Grey Trust*

Wal-Mart
Waterford Glass/
Wedgewood China

Xerox
Yuk Yuks

Zenith

Notes:
N = 101
* = missing some years

Notes

1 INTRODUCTION: HOW ORGANIZATIONAL DECISIONS ARE MADE

1 The major studies in this field are Blau and Schoenherr (1971), Burns and Stalker (1971), Chandler (1962), Lawrence and Lorsch (1967) and Woodward (1969). For a review and history of the findings of the 'contingency' literature, see Mansfield (1986) and Mintzberg (1979). Structural and contextual variables are distinguished in a variety of ways in the literature. See Kimberly and Rottman (1987) and Pfeffer (1982: 149).

2 Some studies of organizational decision-making focus on internal dynamics rather than outcomes, but that alternative leads to serious difficulties with the definition, measurement, and independence of variables. For a discussion of these problems see Bryman (1988) Dess and Origer (1987), and Pfeffer (1982: Ch. 7). By focusing on outcomes, which can be measured objectively and independently of other factors, those problems are minimized in this analysis. Another advantage in using independent budget measures which conform to relatively standardized accounting conventions, is that they allow us to compare firms across industries and across countries. The data used in this part of the study have not been continued beyond 1982 because changes in reporting requirements in 1983 made that impossible.

3 Another consideration was the fact that the author has much more knowledge about these industries than most others.

4 Age was not included as a variable, largely because of the difficulty of establishing the exact age of the firms. To take one example, Manufacturer's Hanover Corporation was formed in 1968 as a multi-bank holding company, but had been incorporated as the Central Trust of New York in 1873. Similarly, most of the loan companies grew or developed through mergers. The real estate development companies were mainly started as home builders following the Second World War, but many have also expanded or developed through mergers.

5 For a discussion of the rationale for using these operational definitions of the variables, and the consequences of employing alternative measures, see Carroll (1990a). For example, in the organizational theory literature number of staff is used more frequently than assets as an indicator of size. In studies that focus upon performance, however, size is more commonly measured by assets. It is for that reason, and because of particular characteristics of the specific industries included in this study, that assets has been selected as the operational

measure here. Nevertheless, the correlation between size measured by assets and by staff is very strong ($r = 0.94$). The variations in measurement of size and performance and the problems in defining independent non-correlated measures of these variables, are discussed by Lawriwsky (1984).

6   Standardized regression coefficients (or Beta-weights) measure the regression coefficient in standard deviation units. They are used in preference to the unstandardized regression coefficients because my interest is the relative weight of the variables within the model, rather than the absolute effect of any one variable. A beta-weight value of 0.40 is twice as great as one of 0.20 and one half as important as 0.80. The r-square values have been adjusted to deal with the interaction between size and function.

2 THE NOTION OF BIAS

1   The definition is from Pareto *Treatise on General Sociology* as cited in Hofstede (1980: 155).
2   This is similar to the pattern of unexplained variance in the model which is discussed in Chapter 6 (sample II).
3   Any reading of the 'public choice' literature provides extensive empirical support for the validity of assumptions of self-interested behaviour in decision-making. *Cf* Tullock and Wagner (1978).
4   For a summary of the cross-cultural literature see Chapter 4.

3 THE IMPACT OF MANAGERIAL DIFFERENCES

1   The effect of interaction between systemic and managerial bias is discussed in Chapter 5.
2   For obvious reasons the individual preferred to remain anonymous. In the course of carrying out this research a number of individuals within the firms were interviewed and their comments are interspersed throughout the text as illustrations. None of the individuals are identified, although in some cases the name of the firm is given.
3   For a description of the Manny Hanny and Bankers Trust see Martin Meyer, *The Bankers* (1974) and Anthony Sampson, *The Money Lenders* (1981); and for the Royal Bank see Rod McQueen, The *Money Spinners* (1983).
4   The problem of classification becomes more complicated when we move to the broader groupings in Chapter 6 and when dealing with the public sector (Carroll 1990c).
5   In this case someone outside of the senior management, the owners, determined a strategy and structured the organization to implement it, a good example of Chandler's (1962) 'strategy then structure'. Cadillac-Fairview is no longer part of the Bronfman-Brascan group. It is still in the retail property development field (Lem 1992).
6   The F-statistic required for inclusion of the variable is significant at the 0.001 level for both equations. The F-statistic measures the total effect of the variable on the equation while the t-statistic measures only the independent effect of the variable not the interactive effects. The lack of significance of the 't' but the high level of significance of the 'F' indicates that much of the effect of management type is in changing the relationship of the other variables with the

dependent variable. Low values of 't' are also to some extent a function of the statistical behaviour of a dummy variable (Wittinck 1988).

7   Statisticians will note that the explained variation for revenue and expenditure was only 20 per cent for the total sample, so cannot be 60 and 70 per cent when the sample is split. The discrepancy is caused by missing values for management type. There were 15 cases missing out of 374 – four were cases of balanced management. The others are in two firms which would not provide sufficient information about the senior managers in the last years of the study to classify them. One firm had previously been technical management, the other administrative. When they are deleted the figure rises to 73 per cent.

8   The mean levels of changes in income and changes in the rate of return are almost identical for each management type, but for technical managers the standard deviations are four times as high for change in income and three times as high for changes in the rate of return which would support a conclusion that it is income smoothing which is the relevant factor at work.

9   See Lawrisky (1984) for a discussion of this literature.

10 The difference was not significant at the 0.05 level.

11 Annual Report of the First Chicago Bank 1974: 3, and Chairman of the Royal Bank of Canada as cited by David Pyette 'Worth Repeating' *Globe and Mail* Toronto, 20 July, 1986 B3.

4 SYSTEMIC DIFFERENCES: THE ROLE OF CULTURE

1   For a detailed outline of the findings of this literature see C. J. Lammers and D. J. Hickson (eds) (1979) *Organizations alike and unlike: International and inter-institutional studies in the sociology of organizations* London: Routledge, Kegan and Paul.

2   Much of this work is found in the literature on policy networks and policy communities (Atkinson and Coleman, 1992). There was also a volume of the journal *Governance* which addressed 'Policy communities as global phenomena' (1989 2:1).

3   Differences in Work-Related Values, Canada and the US:

Uncertainty Avoidance	48	46
U.A. Controlled for age	55	36
Individualism	80	91
Masculinity	52	62

Figures given are Hofstede's index of the degree to which the value is strongly held (Hofstede 1980: 104, 165, 222, 279).

4   Hofstede (1980) does not identify the organization. Judging from the details he does provide, though, one might guess that it is IBM.

5   These findings are derived from faculty listings in graduate school calendars, 1980–1, at the University of British Columbia, McMaster University, McGill University, the University of Toronto, York University, the University of Waterloo and the University of Western Ontario.

6   The comparison of similar systems in order to identify the causes of differences between them has been a standard methodology for more than a century (Mill 1843: 881–2), but it is far from a perfect means of demonstrating cause–effect relationships. No matter how similar two systems may be, we always find more than one remaining difference which might account for the difference in the

dependent variable. In this study the characteristics of the specific industries that are studied, and the criteria used to define the sampling frame from which the sample was selected, are intended to control for at least the most obvious alternatives to the degree of systemic conservatism.

7 The levels of economic development, living standards and patterns of growth were similar for the two countries over the period. This similarity in economic performance can be attributed largely to the linkages between the two economies and the dominance of the American economy in Canada (Economic Council of Canada 1981: 6). For a comparison of the two economies see OECD Country Reports for Canada and the United States for the years in question.

8 The differences in the adjusted r-square values between the two equations are significant at the 0.05 level.

9 Eta is the correlation statistic used with bivariate anova. It is interpreted in the same way as Pearson's r and the eta- square produces the same statistic as the r-square.

10 Of the companies within the sample, Victoria and Grey and National Trust have amalgamated; Canada Permanent was taken over by Canada Trust; and Montreal Trust is now part of a larger trust company structure. Another observation on the differences in the managements of the two countries was the much higher number of vice-presidents, senior vice-presidents, executive vice-presidents, group vice-presidents, and senior executive vice-presidents in the American companies. At Manufacturers-Hanover in 1981 there were some 500 vice-presidents and 69 staff at the executive and senior vice-president level. The Canadian bank which is of a similar size, the CIBC, had 47 vice-presidents and 27 at the executive and senior vice-president level (14 of whom were in their US operation). The highest number of such positions in any Canadian company in the sample was at the Royal Bank with 134 vice-presidents and 38 senior and executive vice-presidents.

11 As with management type and management change, there is some possibility that ownership may also be related to the size of board. Closely held or owner-managed firms would be expected to have a smaller board than widely held firms. When size of board is correlated with ownership, however, there is not a significant relationship. Nor is there any apparent pattern by size within the sector groupings. These findings are not consistent with Clement's (1977) larger study that found that Canadian boards were on average smaller than those in the US. It should be noted, however, that his sample covered dominant corporations in all sectors in Canada, and did not exclude American-owned companies and subsidiaries, which represented a large grouping within his sample.

5 MANAGEMENT TYPE, PERFORMANCE AND VIABILITY

1 The Canada and the United States 'Free Trade Agreement' went into effect 1 January, 1989.

2 Both internal and external measures of the external environment were tested. The internal one, unique to each firm, is its own rate of revenue change. The external indicators of the state of the economy as a whole are the annual rate of growth or decrease in the Gross Domestic Product, and the year-to-year change in the Consumer Price Index (CPI). The results of each of the measures was very similar and the pattern between the four groups remained consistent for

each of them. In computing the measures of the state of the environment, a situation in which the current year was equal to or worse than the previous one on any of the three measures was considered to be an 'unfavourable' environment. While these results remained statistically significant, the number of categories is too large to economically display the full results.

3 Cousins, Nu-West and Daon all experienced such changes; as did First Chicago, the Continental Illinois and the Bank of Montreal.

4 'Experiencing financial difficulty' is used as a euphemism for firms which were near bankruptcy, had to be bailed out, had filed for bankruptcy protection or had experienced losses which were so severe as to make the survival of the organization doubtful.

5 These were the Report by James Morrison into the Affairs of Greymac, Seaway and Crown Trust; the Cody Inquiry into the Principal Group and the Estey Inquiry into the fall of the Canadian Commercial and Northland Banks (Morrison 1983; Alberta 1990; Estey 1986).

6 If newspaper accounts are correct, Olympia and York had sufficient changes of personnel during the late 1980s to constitute a shift from technical to administrative management. The firm is currently under bankruptcy protection in three countries.

6 THE BIAS OF MANAGEMENT

1 The primary source of information in this chapter was interviews with executives or company profiles in *Fortune* magazine from January 1985 to September 1989. During that period any article which provided sufficient information to classify the management or the senior management and the success of the company was included. In addition, the Toronto *Globe and Mail* 'Report on Business' during the same period regularly contained profiles on managers and their companies. These are the companies which provide the basis for the analysis. Additional information was obtained from company annual reports, studies of specific industries, government inquiries in both Canada and the United States and, in a few cases, personal interviews. Specific citations are given in the text.

2 The quality control function is a particularly interesting one in terms of its classification. It is concerned exclusively with the technical sub-system but is both a control function, and a linking function which interprets to the technical sub-system quality demands transmitted from the environment.

3 The typical manager is male. Within this study *all* senior managers, not only bank managers, were male.

4 Urwick spends considerable time on the role of staff in carrying out administrative functions and on how they report to and relate to the operational staff within the organization.

5 The definition of what constituted a successful or unsuccessful firm was based upon *Fortune*'s assessment, usually telegraphed by the language in the title of the article: see note 6 below, for example.

6 Quotations are as follows: 'Those High Flying Pepsico Managers' (*Fortune*, 10 April 1989); John Demont, 'Sharp's Luxury Empire' (*Macleans*, 5 June 1989: 32); Alex Taylor III, 'Keeping the Fires Lit under the Innovator', (*Fortune*, 28 March 1988); and William E. Sheeline, 'Making them Rich Down Home' (*Fortune*, 15 August 1988).

8 E.F. Hutton was a prominent investment brokerage firm in the United States which was caught contravening banking regulations (Fromson 1988). Principal Trust was a Canadian loans and trust company which became insolvent, and it transpired that it was 'buying short and selling long', a practice which for lending institutions is not only imprudent but illegal.

8 Based upon Annual Reports and interviews with Nu-West executives cited previously.

9 This case also provides an example of the iterative decision-making process within the model. The public outcry against rapidly increasing costs, despite the industry's claim that such increases were necessary, was very similar to what had happened when rents began increasing rapidly in the mid-1970s. The response was the same. A review process was established, and set maximum allowable insurance rate increases. In 1990, however, yet another electoral upheaval produced a social democratic provincial government committed to providing automobile insurance through the public sector. This time the industry lobbied early and hard. Despite successful public automobile insurance programmes in three provinces, the industry managed to create a public perception of a certainty of massive job losses and rising insurance rates. The government backed away from its commitment.

7 OVERCOMING THE BIAS OF MANAGEMENT

1 The outside shareholder was the Seagram Bronfmans. The firm was rated as one of the 'successful' firms in the previous chapter. Ironically, although Blair is no longer associated with the company, it remains a 'successful' company. Blair's departure had the effect of changing it from an administrative/technical management type to a balanced management type.

2 Upon his retirement he was replaced by a more administratively orientated manager, Jack Cockwell, who is considered to be a 'financial genius' (Noble 1992).

3 Many cases of balanced management appeared to be a coincidental or passing phase, a circumstance also found in public organizations (Carroll 1990c).

8 MUST BIAS PERSIST?

1 Tom Peters, himself, has now determined that many of the prescriptions contained within *In Pursuit of Excellence* were wrong.

Bibliography

Aaker, David A. and Jacobson, Robert (1987) 'The Role of Risk in Explaining Differences in Profitability' *Academy of Management Journal* 30: 277–96.

Abell, Peter (1975) *Organizations as Bargaining and Influence Systems*, London: Heinemann Education Books.

Aberbach, Joel D., Putman, Robert D. and Rockman, Bert A. (1981) *Bureaucrats and Politicians in Western Democracies*, Cambridge, Mass.: Harvard University Press.

Adler, Nancy J. (1983a) 'Cross-Cultural Management Research: The Ostrich and the Trend', *Academy of Management Review* 8: 226–32.

—— (1983b) 'A Typology of Management Studies Involving Culture', *Journal of International Business Studies* Fall: 29–47.

Adrien, Charles R. and Press, Charles (1968) 'Decision Costs in Coalition Formation', *American Political Science Review* 62: 556–63.

Ajiferuke, M. and Boddewyn, J. (1970) 'Culture and Other Explanatory Variables in Comparative Management Studies', *Academy of Management Journal* 13: 153–63.

Alberta, Government of (1990) *Report by William Cody into the Principal Group of Companies*, Edmonton: Government of Alberta.

Aldine, Goran (1990) *Agency and Organization*, London: Sage.

Alexis, Marcus and Wilson, Charles Z. (1967) *Organizational Decision-Making*, Englewood Cliffs, N.J.: Prentice-Hall.

Allen, Harry T. (1966) 'An Empirical Test of Choice and Decision Postulates in the Cyert and March Behavioral Theory of the Firm', *Administrative Science Quarterly* 2: 405–13.

Allen, M.P. and Panian, S.K. (1982) 'Power, Performance and Succession in Large Organizations', *Administrative Science Quarterly* 27: 538–47.

Almond, Gabriel and Verba, Sidney (1965) *The Civic Culture*, Toronto: Little Brown and Co.

Amihud, Yakas, Kamin, Jacoby and Ronen, Joshua (1983) 'Managerialism, "Ownershipism" and Risk', *Journal of Banking and Finance* 7: 189–96.

Amour, Leslie and Trott, Elizabeth (1981) *The Faces of Reason: An Essay on Philosophy and Culture in English Canada*, Waterloo, Ontario: Wilfred Laurier University Press.

Anderson, Theodore R. and Warkov, S. (1961) 'Organizational Size and Functional Complexity: A Study of Administration in Hospitals', *American Sociological Review* 26: 23–7.

Armstrong, John A. (1973) *The European Administrative Elite*, Princeton, N.J.: Princeton University Press.

Arsteinsen, Barbara (1987) 'Enfield May Be Conservative, But its Growth is Not', *Globe and Mail*, 15 September: B5.

Atkinson, Jay (1977) *The Structure of Cost in the Savings and Loan Industry* (Research Working Paper, No. 67), Washington, D.C.: FHLBB.

Atkinson, Michael M. and Robert A. Nigol. (1988) 'Selecting Policy Instruments: Neo-Institution and Rational Choice Interpretations of Automobile Insurance in Ontario', paper presented to the Canadian Political Science Association, Windsor, Ontario.

Atkinson, Michael M. and Coleman, William D. (1985) 'Bureaucrats and Politicians in Canada: An Examination of the Political Administration Model', *Comparative Political Studies* 18 (1): 58–80.

—— (1992) 'Policy Networks, Policy Communities and the Problems of Governance', *Governance* 5: 154–80.

Baar, Ellen and Makabe, Tomako (1988) 'Bureaucratic and Flexible Structures: The Transition from American to Japanese Management', paper presented to Canadian Sociology Association, Windsor, Ontario.

Bachrach, Peter and Bartz, Morton S. (1962) 'Two Faces of Power', *American Political Science Review* 56: 947–52.

Baldwin, William L. (1964) 'The Motives of Managers, Environmental Restraints and the Theory of Managerial Enterprise', *Quarterly Journal of Economics* 78: 238–56.

Barnard, Chester (1938) *The Functions of the Executive*, Cambridge, Mass.: Harvard University Press.

Barney, Jay B. (1986) 'Organizational Culture: Can It Be a Source of Sustained Competitive Advantage', *Academy of Management Review* 11: 656–65.

Baxter, Vern (1988) 'The process of change in public organizations', *Sociological Quarterly* 30(2): 283–304.

Becker, Theodore M. and Stern, Robert N. (1973) 'Professionalism, Professionalization and Bias in the Commercial Human Relations Consulting Operations: A Survey Analysis', *Journal of Business* 46: 230–57.

Bell, D. and Tepperman, L. (1979) *The Roots of Disunity*, Toronto: McClelland and Stewart.

Bendor, Jonathan and Moe, Terry M. (1985) 'An Adaptive Model of Bureaucratic Politics', *American Political Science Review* 79: 755–74.

Bennis, Warren and Nanus, Burt (1985) *Leaders: The Strategies for Taking Charge*, New York: Harper & Row.

Bell, Norman (1985) 'Professional values and Organizational Decision Making', *Administration and Society* 17(1): 21–60.

Bertin, Oliver (1992) 'US dairy challenge for management', *Globe and Mail* 11 September: B2.

Best, Barbara and Shortell, Ann (1988) *The Brass Ring: Power, Influence and the Brascan Empire*, Toronto: Random House Canada Ltd.

Binhammer, H.H. and Williams, Jane (1976) *Deposit-taking Institutions: Innovation and the Process of Change*, Ottawa: Economic Council of Canada.

Blau, Peter M. and Schoenherr, Richard (1971) *The Structure of Organizations*, New York: Basic Books.

Bozeman, Barry and Slusher, E. Allen (1979) 'Scarcity and Organizational Stress in Public Organizations', *Administration and Society* 11: 335–55.

Bourne, L.S. (1981) *The Geography of Housing*, London: Edward Arnold.

Braybrooke, David and Lindblom, Charles (1963) *A Strategy of Decision*, New York: Free Press.

Brown, M. Craig (1982) 'Administrative Succession and Organizational Performance', *Administrative Science Quarterly*: 28: 1–16.

Brunsson, Nils (1985) *Irrational Organization: Irrationality as a Basis of Organizational Action and Change*, Bath, UK: Bath Press.

Bryman, A. (1984) 'Organizational Studies and the Concept of Rationality', *Journal of Management Studies* 21: 29–44.

—— (ed.) (1988) *Doing Research in Organizations*, London: Routledge.

—— (1988) 'Introduction: 'inside' accounts and social research in organizations', in A. Bryman (ed.) *Doing Research in Organizations*, London: Routledge.

Burns, Tom (ed.) (1969) *The Industrial Man*, Baltimore: Penguin Books.

Burns, Tom and Stalker, G.M. (1971) *The Management of Innovation*, London: Tavistock Publications.

Burrough, Bryan and Helyar, John (1989) *Barbarians at the Gate: The Fall of RJR Nabisco*, New York: HarperCollins.

Business International Research Report (1987) *Restructuring and Turnaround: Experiences in Corporate Renewal*, Geneva: Business International, SA.

Cameron, Kim S., Sutton, Robert I. and Whetten, David A. (eds) (1988) *Readings in Organizational Decline*, Cambridge, Mass.: Ballinger.

—— (1988) 'Issues in Organizational Decline' in Kim S. Cameron, *et al.* (eds) *Readings in Organizational Decline*, Cambridge, Mass.: Ballinger.

Campbell, Colin (1983) *Governments Under Stress: Political Executives and Key Bureaucrats in Washington, London and Ottawa*, Toronto: University of Toronto Press.

Campbell, Colin and Szablowski, George J. (1979) *The Superbureaucrats: Structure and Behavior in Central Agencies*, Toronto: McMillan of Canada.

Canada (1978) *Report of the Royal Commission on Corporate Concentration* (Bryce Commission), Ottawa: Minister of Supply and Services.

—— (1988) *Report of the Auditor-General for Canada*, Ottawa: Ministry of Supply and Services.

Carlisle, Arthur Elliot (1966) 'The Effect of Cultural Differences on Managerial and Industrial Relations Policies and Practices: A Study of U.S. controlled Companies Operating in English and French Canada', Ph.D. dissertation University of Michigan, Ann Arbor Michigan.

Carroll, B.W. (1986) 'Canadian Housing Agencies and Their Management', Paper presented to the Department of Consumer Studies, University of Guelph, April.

—— (1987) 'Size, Technology and Response to Environmental Change in the Residential Construction Industry', paper presented to the Department of Consumer Studies, University of Guelph, November.

—— (1988) 'Market Concentration in a Geographically Segmented Market', *Canadian Public Policy* 14: 295–306.

—— (1990a) 'Systemic Conservatism in North American Organizations', *Organization Studies* 9: 413–33.

—— (1990b) 'Housing Policy' in R. Loreto and T. Price (eds) *Urban Policy Problems: A Canadian Perspective*, Toronto: McLelland and Stewart.

—— (1990c) 'Politics and Administration: A Trichotomy', *Governance* 3: 345–66.

—— (1991) 'The Canadian Bureaucratic Elite: Some Evidence of Change', *Canadian Public Administration* 34(2): 359–72.

Carroll, Barbara W. and Joypaul, S. K. (1993) 'The Mauritian Bureaucratic Elite since Independence: Lessons for Developing and Developed Countries', *International Review of Administrative Sciences* 58(3): 403–20.

Carroll, Glenn R. (ed.) (1988a) *Ecological Models of Organizations*, Cambridge, Mass.: Ballinger.

—— (1988b) 'Organizational Ecology in Theoretical Perspective' in Glenn R. Carroll (ed.) *Ecological Models of Organizations*, Cambridge, Mass.: Ballinger.

Carroll, Terrance G. (1984) 'Secularization and States of Modernity', *World Politics* 36: 262–82.

Carter, Eugene (1971) 'The Behavioral Theory of the Firm and Top Level Corporate Decisions', *Administrative Science Quarterly* 16: 413–31.

Cartwright, T. and Wekerle, G. (1978) 'An Evaluation of Risk Assessment and Management in the Condominium Market', Toronto: C.M.H.C.

Cawson, Alan, Morgan, Kevin, Webber, Douglas, Holmes, Peter and Stevens, Anne (1990) *Hostile Brothers: Competitions and Closure in the European Electronics Industry*, Oxford: Clarendon Press.

Chandler, Alfred E. (1962) *Strategy and Structure*, Cambridge, Mass.: MIT Press.

Chandler, Alfred E. and Daems, Hermann (eds) (1980) *Managerial Hierarchies: Comparative Perspectives on the Rise of the Modern Industrial Enterprise*, Cambridge, Mass.: Harvard University Press.

Chase, Katherine (1986) 'National Banking: A comparison of policy towards nationwide banking and concentration of banking markets in Canada and the U.S.', *Policy Studies Journal* 14: 641–57.

Child, John (1972) 'Organizational Structure, Environment and Performance: The Role of Strategic Choice', *Sociology* 7: 1–20.

—— (1974) 'Managerial and Organizational Factors Associated with Company Performance', *Journal of Management Studies* 11: 175–246.

Child, John and Kieser, Alfred (1981) 'The Development of Organizations over Time' in Paul C. Nystrom and William H. Starbuck (eds) *Handbook of Organizations* Volume 1, Oxford: OUP.

Child, John and Tayeb, M. (1982–3) 'Theoretical Perspectives on Cross-National Organization', *International Studies of Management and Organization* 12: 23–70.

Clark, Robert C. (1985) 'Changes in the U.S. Financial System', in Jacob S. Ziegel, Leonard Waverman and David W. Conklin (eds) *Canadian Financial Institutions: Changing the Regulatory Environment*, Toronto: Ontario Economic Council.

Clarke, Ian M. (1985) *The Spatial Organisation of Multinational Corporations*, New York: St. Martins.

Clement, Wallace (1977) *Continental Corporate Power: Economic Linkages between Canada and the United States*, Toronto: McClelland and Stewart.

Coates, Robert and Updegaff, David E. (1973) 'The Relationship between Organizational Size and the Administrative Component of Banks', *Journal of Business* 46: 576–88.

Cohen, Kalman J. and Cyert, Richard M. (1965) *Theory of the Firm: Resource Allocation in a Market Economy*, Englewood Cliffs, N.J.: Prentice-Hall.

—— (1974) 'Strategy: Formulation, Implementation and Monitoring', *Journal of Business* 46: 349–67.

Cohen, Michael D., March, James G., and Olsen, Johan P. (1972) 'A Garbage Can Model of Organizational Choice', *Administrative Science Quarterly* 7: 1–25.

Coleman, William D. (1988) *Business and Politics*, Montreal: McGill–Queens University Press.

Common, Richard, Flynn, Norman, and Mellon, Elizabeth (1992) *Managing Public Services: Competition and decentralization*, London: Butterworth-Heinemann.

Conference Board, The (1973) *Organization and Control of International Operations*, New York: The Conference Board.

Crozier, Michel (1964) *The Bureaucratic Phenomenon*, Chicago: University of Chicago Press.

Cummings, L.L. (1983) 'The Logics of Management', *Academy of Management Review* 8: 532–9.

Cyert, Richard M. and March, James G. (eds) (1963) *The Behavioral Theory of the Firm*, Englewood Cliffs, N.J.: Prentice-Hall.

Cyert, Richard M. (1978) 'The Management of Universities of Constant or Decreasing Size', *Public Administration Review* 38: 334–49.

Czarnlawska-Joerges, Barbara and Wolff, Rolf (1991) 'Leaders, Managers and Entrepreneurs: On and Off the Organizational Stage', *Organization Studies* 12(4): 529–46.

Czarnlawska-Joerges, Barbara (1992) *Exploring Complex Organizations*, London:Sage.

Daft, Richard L. (1983) *Organization Theory and Design*, St. Paul, Minn.: West Publishing Co.

Dearborn, Dewitt C. and Simon, Herbert R. (1958) 'Selective Perception: A Note on the Departmental Identification of Executives', *Sociometry* 21: 140–4.

Demont, John (1989a) 'The Tough Tycoons', *Maclean's* 6 February: 32–40.

—— (1989b) 'Sharp's Luxury Empire', *Maclean's* 5 June: 30–6.

Derlien, Hans-Ulrich (1992) 'Observations on the State of Comparative Administration Research in Europe – Rather Comparable than Comparative', *Governance* 5: 279–311.

Dess, Gregory G. and Origer, Nancy K. (1987) 'Environment, Structure and Consensus in Strategy Formulation: A Conceptual Integration', *Academy of Management Review* 12(2): 313–30.

Downing, Paul B. and Brady, Gordon L. (1979) 'Constrained Self-Interest and the Formation of Public Policy', *Public Choice* 34: 15–28.

Downs, Anthony (1967) *Inside Bureaucracy*, Boston: Little Brown.

Dumaine, Brian (1989) 'Those Hyflying Pepsico Managers', *Fortune* 10 April.

Dunbar, Roger L. (1971) 'Budgeting for Control', *Administrative Science Quarterly* 16: 83–90.

Dunbar, Roger L. and Goldberg, Walter M., (1978) 'Crisis Development and Strategic Response in European Corporations', in C.F. Smart and W.T. Stanbury (eds), *Studies on Crisis Management*, Toronto: Butterworth.

Dunleavy, Patrick (1981) *The Politics of Mass Housing in Britain 1945–1975: A Study of Corporate Power and Professional Influence in the Welfare State*, Oxford: Clarendon Press.

—— (1989) 'The Architecture of the British Central State', *Public Administration* 76: 391–417.

Dutton, Jane E. and Ottensmeyer, Edward (1987) 'Strategic Issues Management Systems: Forms, Function and Contexts', *Academy of Management Review* 12: 355–65.

Ealau, Jacques (1964) 'Logics of Rationality in Unanimous Decision Making' in Carl J. Friedrich (ed.) *Rational Decision*, New York: Atherton Press.

Eccles, Robert (1981) 'The Quasifirm in the Construction Industry', *Journal of Economic Behavior and Organization* 3: 235–55.

Economic Council of Canada (1982) *Intervention and Efficiency: A Study of Government Credit and Credit Guarantees to the Private Sector*, Ottawa: Canada, Ministry of Supply and Services.

—— (1981) *Eighteenth Annual Review* Ottawa: Economic Council of Canada.

Eichler, Ned (1982) *The Merchant Builders*, Cambridge, Mass.: MIT Press.

Enchin, Harvey (1986) 'Expansion of Yuk Yuks Clubs is no Laughing Matter', *Globe and Mail* 10 February: B5.

Estey, The Honourable William B. (1986) *Report of the Inquiry into the Collapse of the CCB and Northland*, Ottawa: Minister of Supply and Services, Canada.

Everett, J.E., Sterling, B.W. and Lonton, P.A. (1982) 'Some Evidence for an International Management Culture', *Journal of Management Science* 19: 153–62.

Fayol, Henry (1937) 'The Administrative Theory in the State' in Luther Gulick and L. Urwick, (eds) *Papers on the Science of Administration*, New York: Institute of Public Administration.

Feschuk, Scott (1991) 'John Labatt spinning off $2-billion dairy business', *Globe and Mail* 11 September: B1.

—— (1992) 'Inglis turnaround a "heroic" effort', *Globe and Mail* 17 August: B1.

Finer, Herman (1941) 'Administrative Responsibility in Democratic Government', *Public Administration Review* 1: 335–50.

Fombrun, Charles J. (1986) 'Structural Dynamics within and between Organizations', *Administrative Science Quarterly* 31: 403–21.

Ford, Jeffrey D. (1981) 'Departmental Context and Formal Structure as Constraints on Leader Behavior', *Academy of Management Journal* 24: 274–88.

Ford, Jeffrey D. and Baucus, David C. (1987) 'Organizational Adaptation to Performance Downturns: An Interpretation-Based Perspective', *Academy of Management Review* 12(2): 366–80.

Frederickson, James W. (1986) 'The Strategic Decision Process and Organizational Structure', *Academy of Management Review* 11(2): 280–97.

Freeman, John and Hannan, Michael T. (1975) 'Growth and Decline Processes in Organizations', *American Sociological Review* 40: 215–28.

French, Richard D. (1980) *How Ottawa Decides*, Toronto: James Lorimer & Company.

Frieder, Larry A. (1980) *Commercial Banking and Holding Company Acquisitions*, Ann Arbor, Mich.: UMI Research Press.

Friedrich, Carl J. (ed.) (1964) *Rational Decision*, New York: Atherton Press.

Fromson, Brett (1988) 'The Slow Death of E.F. Hutton', *Fortune* 20 February: 82–8.

Fry, Louis W. (1982) 'Technology–Structure Research: Three Critical Issues', *Academy of Management Journal* 25: 532–52.

Gibb, C.A. (1954) 'Leadership' in G. Lindley (ed.) *Handbook of Social Psychology*, Reading, Mass.: Addison-Wesley.

Gibbins, Robert (1989) 'Campeau Divestment Going Well', *Globe and Mail* 14 October: B1.

Gibbins, Roger (1982) *Regionalism: Territorial Politics in Canada and the United States*, Toronto: Butterworth.

Gibbons, Ann (1992) 'Ding-Dong, Avon smalling', *Globe and Mail*, 18 August: B18.

Goldberg, Michael A. and Mercer, John (1986) *The Myth of the North American City: Continentalism Challenged*, Vancouver: University of British Columbia Press.

Goldenberg, Susan (1981) *Men of Property: The Canadian Developers who are Buying America*, Toronto: Personal Library.

Goodin, Robert and Waldner, Ilmar (1979) 'Thinking Big, Thinking Small and Not Thinking at All', *Public Policy* 27: 1–24.

Gordon, Marcy (1988) 'Airlines Now Seeking Wall Street Barnstormers', *Globe and Mail* 1 November: B19.

Goyens, Chrys and Turowetz, Allan (1986) *Lions in Winter*, Scarborough, Ont.: Prentice-Hall.

Graham, J.F. *et al.* (1962) 'The Role of the Trust and Loan Companies in the Canadian Economy', London, Ontario: School of Business Administration, University of Western Ontario.

Grebler, Leo (1973) *Large Scale Housing and Real Estate Firms*, New York: Praeger.

Greiner, Larry E. (1972) 'Evolution and Revolution as Organizations Grow', *Harvard Business Review* 50: 37–46.

Grochla, Erwin and Szyperski, Norbert (eds) (1979) *Information Systems and Organizational Structure*, Berlin: De Gruyter.

Gruber, Judith (1984) *Controlling Bureaucracy*, Berkeley, Calif.: University of California Press.

Grusky, Oscar (1961) 'Corporate Size, Bureaucratization and Managerial Succession', *American Journal of Sociology* 67: 261–9.

Gulick, Luther (1937) 'Notes on the Theory of Organization', in Luther Gulick and L. Urwick (eds) *Papers on the Science of Administration*, New York: Institute of Public Administration.

Gulick, Luther and Urwick, L. (eds) (1937) *Papers on the Science of Administration*, New York: Institute of Public Administration.

Hage, Jerald (1980) *Theories of Organization: Form, Process and Transformation*, Toronto: J. Wiley and Son.

Halberstam, David (1986) *The Reckoning*, New York: Avon Books.

Hall, Douglas T. and Mansfield, Roger (1971) 'Organizational and Individual Response to External Stress', *Administrative Science Quarterly* 16: 533–47.

Hall, R. I. (1976) 'A System Pathology of an Organization: The Rise and Fall of the Old Saturday Evening Post', *Administrative Science Quarterly* 21: 185–211.

Hambrick, Donald C. and Mason, Phyllis A. (1984) 'Upper Echelons: The Organization as a Reflection of its Top Managers', *Academy of Management Review* 9(2): 193–206.

Hannaway, J. (1987) 'Supply Creates Demand: An Organizational Process View of Administrative Expansion', *Journal of Policy Analysis and Management* 7(1): 118–34.

Harbison, Frederick and Myers, Charles A. (1959) *Management in the Industrial World: An International Analysis*, New York: McGraw-Hill.

Harrison, J.R., Torres, D.L. and Kulalis, S. (1988) 'The Changing of the Guard: Turnover and Structural Change in Top Management Positions', *Administrative Science Quarterly* 33: 211–32.

Hector, Gary (1984) 'Bankers Trust takes on Wall Street', *Fortune* 9 January: 104–7.

Hedburg, Bo L.T., Nystrom, Paul C. and Starbuck, William H. (1976) 'Camping on Seesaws: Prescriptions for a Self-Designing Organization', *Administrative Science Quarterly* 21: 41–65.

Henkoff, Ronald (1988) 'This Cat is Acting Like a Tiger', *Fortune* 19 December.

Herzberg, Frederick (1968) 'One More Time: How Do You Motivate Employees?', *Harvard Business Review* 46: 53–62.

Higgins, D.J.H. (1986) *Local and Urban Politics in Canada*, Toronto: Gage.

Hill, C.W.L. (1984) 'Organizational Structure, The Development of the Firm and Business Behavior', in J.F. Pickering and T.A.J. Cockerill (eds) *The Economic Management of the Firm*, Deddington, Oxford: Philip Allan Publishers.

Hinings, Charles R. (1979) 'Continuities in the Study of Organizations', in Cornelius J. Lammers and David J. Hickson (eds) *Organizations Alike and Unlike: international and inter-institutional studies in the sociology of organizations*, London: Routledge and Kegan.

Hirschman, Albert O. (1970) *Exit, Voice and Loyalty*, Cambridge, Mass.: Harvard University Press.

Hofstede, Geert (1980) *Culture's Consequences: International Differences in Work Related Values*, Beverly Hills, Calif.: Sage.

Holsti, Ole R. (1978) 'Limitation of Cognitive Abilities in the Face of Crisis', in C.F. Smart and W.T. Stanbury (eds) *Studies on Crisis Management*, Toronto: Butterworth.

Huey, John (1989) 'The New Power in Black & Decker', *Fortune* 21 January.

Jaeger, A.M. (1982–3) 'Contrasting Control Modes in the Multinational Corporation: Theory, Practice and Implications', *International Studies of Management and Organization* 12: 59–82.

Jain, H.C. and Kanungo, R.N. (eds) (1977) *Behavioral Issues in Management: The Canadian Context*, Toronto: McGraw-Hill.

Jamieson, Ian M. (1982–3) 'The Concept of Culture and its Relevance for an Analysis of Business Enterprises in Different Societies', *International Studies of Management and Organization* 12 (Winter): 71–105.

Janis, Irving L. (1972) *Victims of Groupthink: A Psychological Study of Foreign Policy Decisions and Fiascoes*, Boston: Houghton-Mifflin Co.

Janowitz, Morris (1960) *The Professional Soldier*, Glencoe, Ill.: The Free Press.

Jenkins, W.I. (1978) *Policy Analysis: A Political and Organizational Perspective*, London: Martin Robertson.

Jenner, S.R. (1982) 'Analyzing Cultural Stereotypes in Multinational Business: U.S. and Australia', *Journal of Management Science* 19: 397–404.

Jessee, Michael A. and Seelig, Steven A. (1977) *Bank Holding Companies and the Public Interest*, Lexington, Mass.: Lexington Books.

Johnson, Andrew and D'aigneault, Jean (1988) 'Liberal "Chefs de Cabinets" in Quebec: Keeping Politics in Policy-Making'. *Canadian Journal of Political Science*: 31–4: 483–500.

Jonsson, Sten A. and Lundin, Rolf A. (1969) 'Myths and Wishful Thinking as Management Tools', *Academy of Management Journal* 12: 157–170.

Katz, Daniel and Kahn, Robert L. (1978) *The Social Psychology of Organizations* 2nd edn, New York: J. Wiley and Sons.

Kaufman, Herbert (1976) *Are Government Organizations Immortal?*, Washington, D.C.: Brookings Institution.

—— (1985) *Time, Chance and Organizations: Natural Selection in Perilous Environments*, Chatham, N.J.: Chatham House.

Kernaghan, Kenneth (1984) 'The Conscience of the Bureaucrat', *Canadian Public Administration* 27: 576–91.

Khandwalla, Pradip N. (1977) 'Styles of Management and the Environment: Some

Findings', in H.C. Jain and R.N. Kanungo (eds) *Behavioral Issues in Management: The Canadian Context*, Toronto: McGraw-Hill.

Kiebel, Walter (1989) 'Corporate Strategy for the 1990's', *Fortune* 29 February: 39–43.

Kilmann, Ralph H. (1989) *Managing Beyond the Quick Fix* Berkeley, Calif.: Jossey-Bass.

Kimberly, James R. and Rottman, David B. (1987) 'Environment, Organization and Effectiveness: A Biographical Approach', *Journal of Management Studies* 24: 595–622.

Kirkland, Richard (1989) 'Grand Met's Recipe for Pillsbury', *Fortune* 13 March.

Kmenta, Jan (1986) *Elements of Econometrics*, New York: Macmillan.

Kolarska, L. and Aldrich H. (1980) 'Exit, Voice and Silence: Consumers and Managers' Response to Organizational Decline', *Organizational Studies* 1: 41–58.

Kold, R.W. (1981) 'Affiliated and Independent: Two Behavioral Regimes', *Journal of Banking and Finance* 5: 523–37.

Kriesberg, Louis (1962) 'Careers, Organization Size, and Succession', *American Journal of Sociology* 68: 355–9.

Kwast, Myron L. and Rose, John T. (1982) 'Pricing, Operating Efficiency and Profitability among Large Commercial Banks', *Journal of Banking and Finance* 6: 233–54.

Laband, David N. (1983) 'Federal Budget Cuts: The Bureaucrats Trim the Meat, Not the Fat', *Public Choice* 41: 311–5.

Lammers, Cornelius J. and Hickson, David J. (eds) (1979) *Organizations Alike and Unlike: international and inter-institutional studies in the sociology of organizations*, London: Routledge and Kegan Paul.

—— (1979) 'Are Organizations Culture Bound?', in Cornelius J. Lammers and David J. Hickson (eds) *Organizations Alike and Unlike: International and Interinstitutional Studies in the Sociology of Organizations*, London: Routledge and Kegan Paul.

Lamont, Carol J. (1988) 'The New J.P. Morgans', *Fortune* 29 February: 44–53.

Landau, Martin (1973) 'On the Concept of a Self-Correcting Organization', *Public Administration Review* 33: 533–43.

Lawrence, Paul R. and Lorsch, Jay W. (1967) *Organizations and Environment: Managing Differentiation and Change*, Cambridge, Mass.: Harvard University Press.

Lawriwsky, Michael L. (1984) *Corporate Structure and Performance: The Role of Owners, Managers and Markets*, London: Croom Helm.

Leemans, A.F. (ed.) (1976) *The Management of Change in Government*, The Hague: Martin Nijhoff.

Lem, Gail (1992) 'Caution keeps Cadillac on the right road', *Globe and Mail* 8 September: B6.

Lermer, George (1978) *The Performance of Canadian Banks*, Economic Council of Canada Discussion Paper No. 104, Ottawa: Canada, Department of Supply and Services.

Levine, Charles H. (ed.) (1980) *Managing Fiscal Stress*, Chatham, N.J.: Chatham House.

—— (1980) 'More on Cutback Management: Hard Questions for Hard Times', in Charles H. Levine (ed.) *Managing Fiscal Stress*, Chatham, N.J.: Chatham House.

Lijphart, Arendt (1984) *Democracies: Patterns of Majoritarian and Consensus Government in Twenty-One Countries*, Westford, Mass.: Yale University Press.

Lindblom, Charles E. and Cohen, David K. (1958) *Usable Knowledge*, New Haven: Yale University Press.

Lindley, G. (ed.) (1954) *Handbook of Social Psychology*, Reading, Mass.: Addison-Wesley.

Lipset, Seymour Martin (1986) 'Historical Traditions and National Characteristics: A Comparative Analysis of Canada and the United States', *Canadian Journal of Sociology* 11: 113–55.

Lohr, Steve (1989) 'Once Perfect, Waterford–Wedgewood Marriage Now Showing Cracks', *Globe and Mail*, 24 April: B7.

Lord, C.L., Lepper, M.L. and Strack, F. (1975) 'Social Explanation and Social Expectation: The Effect of Real and Hypothetical Explanation Upon Subjective Likelihood', *Journal of Personality and Social Psychology* 35: 817–29.

Lord, C., Ross, L. and Lepper, M.R. (1979) 'Biased Assimilation and Attitude Polarization', *Journal of Personality and Social Psychology* 37: 2098–2109.

Loreto, R. and Price, T. (eds) (1990) *Urban Policy Problems: A Canadian Perspective*, Toronto: McLelland & Stewart.

Lorimer, James (1978) *The Developers*, Toronto: James Lorimer and Co.

Lush, Patricia (1983) 'Reorganization Changes Cadillac-Fairview Image', *Globe and Mail*, 28 March: B1.

McCallum, Anthony (1984) 'Nu-West Sells Voyager Unit to U.S. Firms', *Globe and Mail* 20 July: B1.

McClelland, Hassell H. (1981) *Managing One-Bank Holding Companies*, New York: Praeger.

McCrimmon, K.R. and Wehrung, D.A. (1986) *Taking Risks: The Management of Uncertainty*, New York: The Free Press.

MacDonald, Flora (1980) 'The Minister and the Mandarins' *Policy Options* 1(3): 29–31.

McGregor, Douglas (1960) *The Human Side of Enterprise*, New York: McGraw-Hill.

McKenna, Barrie (1989) 'Domtar Plans Big Staff Cuts in Montreal', *Globe and Mail* 11 October: B1, B5.

McKercher, William R. (ed.) (1983) *The U.S. Bill of Rights and the Canadian Charter of Rights and Freedoms*, Toronto: Ontario Economic Council.

McKinley, W. (1987) 'Complexity and Administrative Intensity: The Case of Declining Organizations', *Administrative Science Quarterly* 32: 87–105.

McMillan, Charles J., Hickson, David J., Hinings, Christopher R. and Schneck, Rodney E. (1973) 'The Structure of Work Organizations Across Societies', *Academy of Management Journal* 16: 555–69.

McQueen, Rod (1983) *The Moneyspinners: The men who control Canada's Banks*, Toronto: Macmillan.

Mack, Ruth P. (1971) *Planning on Uncertainty: Decision-Making in Business and Government Administration*, New York: Wiley and Son.

Madar, Daniel and Richard Stairs (1977) 'Alone on Killers' Row: The Policy Analysis Group and the Department of External Affairs', *International Journal* 32(4): 727–55.

Mannheim, Bilha F. and Moscovits, Nathan (1979) 'Contextual Variables and Bureaucratic Types of Israeli Service Organizations', in Cornelius J. Lammers and David J. Hickson (eds) *Organizations Alike and Unlike: International and Institutional Studies in the Sociology of Organizations*, London: Routledge and Kegan Paul.

Mannheim, Karl (1936) *Ideology and Utopia: An Introduction to the Sociology of Knowledge*, New York: Harcourt, Brace.

Mansfield, Roger (1986) *Company Strategy and Organizational Design*, London: Croom Helm.

March, James G. (1962) 'Business Firms as a Political Coalition', *Journal of Politics* 24: 662–8.

March, James G. and Shapira, Z. (1992) 'Behavioral Decision Theory and Organizational Decision Theory' in Mary Zey (ed.) *Decision-Making: Alternative to Rational Choice Models*, Newbury Park, Calif: Sage.

March, James G. and Simon, Herbert A. (1958) *Organizations*, New York: Wiley and Sons.

Marks, Mitchell Lee (1988) 'The Disappearing Company Man', *Psychology Today* 22(9): 34–42.

Meltsner, Arnold J. (1976) *Policy Analysts in the Bureaucracy*, Berkeley: University of California Press.

Merkle, Judith A. (1980) *Management and Ideology*, Berkeley, Calif.: University of California Press.

Meyer, Alan D. (1982) 'Adapting to Environmental Jolts', *Administrative Science Quarterly* 27: 515–37.

Meyer, John W. and Rowan, Brian (1977) 'Institutionalized Organizations: Formal Structure as Myth and Ceremony', *American Journal of Sociology* 83: 340–63.

Meyer, Marshall W. (1985) *The Limits to Bureaucratic Growth*, The Hague: Van Nostrand.

Meyer, Martin (1974) *The Bankers*, New York: Weybright and Talley.

Michels, Robert (1966) *Political Parties*, New York: Free Press.

Mill, John S. (1843) *A System of Logic* (1973 edition, J.M. Robson, ed.), Toronto: University of Toronto Press.

Millikin, Frances J. (1987) 'Three Types of Perceived Uncertainty about the Environment', *Academy of Management Review* 12: 132–43.

Mintz, Jack M. (1979) *The Measure of Rates of Return in Canadian Banking*, Ottawa: Economic Council of Canada.

Mintzberg, Henry (1979) *The Structuring of Organizations*, Englewood Cliffs, N.J.: Prentice-Hall.

—— (1983) *Power In and Around Organizations*, Englewood Cliffs, N.J.: Prentice-Hall.

—— (1988) 'Remarks', Touraine, Quebec: Canada Centre for Management Development.

Mittelstadt, Martin (1983) 'Exits from CIBC Stir Speculation', *Globe and Mail* 4 January: B5.

—— (1987) 'Continental Illinois Recovers from a Grueling Run', *Globe and Mail* 29 July: B3.

—— (1988) 'Proudly Independent Glen Fed Founded in Depression', *Globe and Mail* 4 August: B2.

Morgan, Glenn (1990) *Organizations in Society*, New York: St. Martin's.

Morrison, James A. (1983) *Report of the Special Examiner of Crown Trust Company, Greyac Trust Company, Seaway Trust Company, Greymac Mortgage Corporation and Seaway Mortgage Corporation to the Honourable Robert G. Elgie, Minister of Consumer and Corporate Relations, Province of Ontario, June 1983*, Toronto: Department of Consumer and Commercial Relations.

Mouzelis, Nico (1968) *Organization and Bureaucracy*, London: Aldine.

Neghandi, Anant R. (1983) 'Cross-Cultural Management Research: Trend and Future Directions', *Journal of International Business Studies* Fall: 17–28.

Nemetz, P., Stanburg, W.T. and Thompson, Fred (1986) 'Social Regulation in Canada: An Overview and Comparison with the American Model', *Political Studies Journal* 14: 580–603.

Newman, Peter (1978) *The Bronfman Dynasty*, Toronto: McClelland and Stewart.

Nightingale, Donald (1977) 'Structure and Organization Theory: An Integration and Cross-Cultural Empirical Test', in H.C. Jain and R.N. Kanungo (eds) *Behavioral Issues in Management: The Canadian Context*, Toronto: McGraw-Hill.

Niskanen, William A. (1971) *Bureaucracy and Representative Government*, Chicago: Aldine/Atherton.

Noble, Kimberley (1989a) 'Enfield President Resigns His Directorship', *Globe and Mail* 2 September: B5.

—— (1989b) 'Canadian Express Kept Enfield in Dark', *Globe and Mail* 4 September: B7.

—— (1992) 'Col. Mike: He did it his way', *Globe and Mail*, 15 September: B1.

Norburn, David (1987) 'Corporate Leaders in Britain and America: A Cross-National Analysis', *International Journal of Business Studies* Fall: 15–32.

Nystrom, Paul C. and Starbuck, William H. (eds) (1981) *Handbook of Organizations* (Vol. 1), Oxford: OUP.

—— (1988) 'To Avoid Organizational Crises, Unlearn' in Kim S. Cameron, Robert I. Sutton and David A. Whitten (eds) *Readings in Organizational Decline*, Cambridge, Mass.: Ballinger.

OECD (1973–1984a) *Country Reports – Canada*, Paris: OECD.

—— (1973–1984b) *Country Reports – U.S.*, Paris: OECD.

Ouchi, William B. (1981) *Theory Z*, Reading, Mass.: Addison-Wesley.

Page, Don (1987) 'Drawing Lessons from a Policy Planning/Analysis Exercise', paper prepared for presentation to the Joint National Meeting of the National Council on Public History and the Society for History in the Federal Government, Washington, D.C., April.

Page, Edward C. (1985) *Political Authority and Bureaucratic Power*, Brighton, UK: Wheatsheaf Books.

Parkinson, C. Northcote (1964) *Parkinson's Law* New York: Ballantine Books.

Parsons, Talcott (ed.) (1947) *Max Weber: The Theory Social and Economic Organization*, New York: Glencoe Free Press.

—— (1949) *The Structure of Social Action*, New York: Glencoe Free Press.

—— (1960) *Structure and Process in Modern Societies*, New York: Glencoe Free Press.

Pasmore, William A. (1988) *Designing Effective Organizations*, New York: John Wiley and Sons.

Perrow, Charles H. (1970) *Organizational Analysis: A Sociological Perspective*, Belmont, Calif.: Wadworth.

Peters, B. Guy (1986) *The Politics of Bureaucracy: A Comparative Perspective* (2nd edn), New York: Longman.

Peters, Thomas J. and Waterman, Robert H. (1982) *In Search of Excellence*, New York: Harper & Row.

Pettigrew, Andrew M. (1973) *The Politics of Organizational Decision-making*, London: Tavistock.

Pfeffer, Jeffrey (1982) *Organizations and Organization Theory*, London: Pitman Books.

Pfeffer, Jeffrey and Davis-Blake, Alison (1986) 'Administrative Succession and organizational Performance: How Administrator Experience Mediates the Succession Effect', *Academy of Management Journal* 19: 72–83.

Pfeffer, Jeffrey and Salancik, Gerald B. (1974) 'Organizational Decision-making as a Political Process: The Case of a University Budget', *Administrative Science Quarterly* 19: 135–51.

—— (1978) *External Control of Organizations*, New York: Harper & Row.

Phidd, R.W. (1988) 'The Reorganization of Finance Ministries and their Role in Policy Formulation: A Case Study of Finance Canada, 1963–1988', paper prepared for the Annual Meeting of the Canadian Political Science Association, Windsor, Ontario.

Philip, Margaret (1989) 'Deadline Looms for Campeau Empire', *Globe and Mail* 14 September 14: B1, and B5.

Pickering, J.F. and Cockerill, T.A.J. (eds) (1984) *The Economic Management of the Firm*, Deddington, Oxford: Philip Allan Publishers.

Pondy, Louis R. (1970) 'Toward a Theory of Internal Resource Allocation', in Mayer N. Zald (ed.) *Power in Organizations*, Nashville, Tenn.: Vanderbilt University Press.

Porter, John (1978) *The Vertical Mosaic*, Toronto: University of Toronto Press.

Porter, Michael (1985) *Competitive Advantage*, New York: Free Press.

Presthus, Robert (1973) *Elite Accommodation in Canadian Politics*, Toronto: Macmillan.

Putman, Robert D., Leonardi, Robert and Nanett, Raffaella (1988) 'Institutional Performance and Political Culture: Some Puzzles about the Power of the Past', *Governance* 1: 221–42.

Ramirez, Anthony (1988) 'The Secret Bomber Bugging Northrup' *Fortune* 14 March: 90–3.

Reich, Robert (1983) *The Next American Frontier*, New York: Fitzhenry & Whiteside.

—— (1987) *Tales of a New America*, New York: Times Books.

Roberts, K.H. (1977) 'On Looking at an Elephant' in Theodore H. Weinshall (ed.) *Culture and Management*, Harmondsworth, Middx: Penguin Books.

Romzek, Barbara S. and Dubnick, Melvin J. (1987) 'Accountability in the Public Sector: Lessons from the Challenger Tragedy', *Public Administration Review* 47: 227–38.

Rowe, James (1984) 'How a Bank Lent Itself to Disaster', *Washington Post* 27 July: A1–2.

Rubin, Irene (1980) 'Universities Under Stress', in Charles H. Levine (ed.) *Managing Fiscal Stress*, Chatham, N.J.: Chatham House.

Sampson, Anthony (1981) *The Money Lenders: Bankers in a Dangerous World*, London: Hodder & Stoughton.

Saporito, Bill (1988a) 'The Tough Cookie at RJR Nabisco, *Fortune* 18 July.

—— (1998b) 'The Fix is in at Home Depot', *Fortune* 29 February: 73–9.

Schreyogg, Georg and Steinman, Horst (1987) 'Strategic Control: A New Perspective', *Academy of Management Review* 12: 91–103.

Schick, Allen G. (1985) 'University Budgeting: Administrative Perspective, Budget Structure and Budget Process', *Academy of Management Review* 10: 794–802.

Schull, Joseph and Gibson, J. Douglas (1982) *The ScotiaBank Story*, Toronto: McMillan of Canada.

Sellers, Patricia (1988a) 'Lessons From T.V.'s New Bosses', *Fortune*, 14 March: 115–30.

—— (1988b) 'How King Kellogg Beat the Blahs', *Fortune* 29 August.

—— (1988c) 'Why Bigger is Badder at Sears', *Fortune* 5 December.

Sharfman, Mark P. (1988) 'Antecedents of Organizational Slack', *Academy of Management Review*, 13(4): 601–14.

Sherman, Stafford (1989) 'The Smutty Story of Cabot Corp', *Fortune* 5 December: 137–40.

Shrwastava, Paul, Mitroff, Ian I. and Alvesson, Mats (1987) 'Non-Rationality in Organizational Acts', *International Studies of Management and Organization* 7: 90–109.

Shull, Fremont A., Delberg, Andre L. and Cumming L.L. (1970) *Organizational Decision-making*, New York: McGraw-Hill.

Simon, Herbert A. (1965) *Administrative Behavior* (2nd edn), Toronto: Collier-Macmillan.

Smart, C.F. and Stanbury, W.T. (eds) (1978) *Studies on Crisis Management*, Toronto: Butterworth.

Smart, Caroline F., Thompson, William A. and Vertinsky, I. (1978) 'Diagnosing Corporate Effectiveness and Susceptibility to Crisis', in Caroline Smart and William T. Stanbury, (eds) *Studies on Crisis Management*, Toronto: Butterworth.

Sonnenfield, Jeffrey (1981) 'Executive Apologies for Price Fixing: Role Biased perceptions of Causality', *Academy of Management Journal* 24: 192–8.

Spellman, Lewis J. (1982) *The Depository Firm and Industry: Theory, History and Regulation*, Orlando: Academic Press.

Starbuck, William H. (1979) 'Information systems for organizations of the future', in Erwin Grochla and Norbert Szyperski (eds) *Information Systems and Organizational Structure*, Berlin: De Gruyter.

Starbuck, William H., Greve, Arent and Hedberg, Bo L.T. (1978) 'Responding to Crisis: Theory and the Experience of European Business', in C.F. Smart and W.T. Stanbury (eds) *Studies on Crisis Management*, Toronto:Butterworth.

Starbuck, William H. and Nystrom, Paul C. (1988) 'To avoid organizational crisis: unlearn', in Kim S. Cameron, Robert I. Sulten and David Whetten (eds) *Readings in Organizational Decline*, Cambridge: Mass.: Ballinger.

Staw, Barry M., Sundelands, Lance E. and Dutton, Jane E. (1981) 'Threat and Rigidity Effects in Organizational Behavior: A Multilevel Analysis', *Administrative Science Quarterly* 26: 501–24.

Stoffman, David (1989) 'Management by Mayhem', *Report on Business Magazine*, May: 42–51.

Stout, Russell, Jr. (1980) *Management or Control?*, Bloomington, Ind.: Indiana University Press.

Strich, Andrew J. (1986) 'Business Interests and Policy Formation: The Steel Industry and Import Policy in Canada and the United States' (unpublished Ph.D dissertation, Queen's University, Kingston).

Sutherland, John W. (1977) *Administrative Decision-making: Extending the Bounds of Rationality*, New York: Van Nostrand Reinhold.

Sutton, Robert I. and Callahan, Anita L. (1988) 'The Stigma of Bankruptcy: Spoiled Organizational Image and Its Management', in Kim S. Cameron, Robert I. Sutton and David A. Whetten (eds), *Readings in Organizational Decline*, Cambridge, Mass.: Ballinger.

Tainio, Risto, Korhomen, J. Polla and Santalainen, Timo J. (1991) 'In Search of Explanations for Bank Performance: Some Finnish Data', *Organization Studies* 12(3): 425–50.

Taylor, Alex (1987) 'G.E.'s Hard Drive at NBC', *Fortune* 16 March.

—— (1988) 'Iacocca's Time of Trouble', *Fortune* 14 March: 79–88.

Theonig, Jean Claude and Freidberg, Erhard (1976) 'The Power of the Field Staff. The Case of the Ministry of Public Works, Urban Affairs and Housing in France', in A.F. Leemans, (ed.) *The Management of Change in Government*, The Hague: Martin Nijhoff.

Thompson, James D. (1967) *Organizations in Action*, Toronto: McGraw-Hill.

Thompson, Victor (1976) *Without Sympathy or Enthusiasm: The Problem of Administrative Compassion*, Chatanooga, Alabama: The University of Alabama Press.

Tullock, Gordon and Wagner, Richard E. (1978) *Policy Analysis and Deductive Reasoning*, Lexington, Mass.: Lexington Books.

Tully, Shawn (1989) 'Nestle shows how to gobble markets', *Fortune* 16 January.

Ullrich, Robert A. and Wieland, George F. (1980) *Organization Theory and Design* (rev. edn), Homewood, Ill.: Richard D. Irwin.

Ungson, Gerardo Rivera, Braunstein, Daniel N. and Hall, Phillip D. (1981) 'Managerial Information Processing: A Research Review', *Administrative Science Quarterly* 26: 116–34.

Urwick, L. (1937) 'Organization as a Technical Problem' in Luther Gulick and L. Urwick (eds) *Papers on the Science of Administration*, New York: Institute of Public Administration.

Vogel, David (1986) *National Styles of Regulation*, Ithaca, N.Y: Cornell University Press.

Watt, Keith (1990) 'Woodsman, Spare that Tree', *Report on Business Magazine* March: 48–55.

Weber, Max (1966), *Max Weber: The Theory of Social and Economic Organization* (translated by A.M. Henderson and Talcott Parsons), New York: Free Press.

Weinshall, Theodore H. (ed.) (1977) *Culture and Management*, Harmondsworth, Middx: Penguin Books.

—— (1977) 'Multinational Corporations – A Total System Approach to Their Role and Measurement', in Theodore D. Weinshall, (ed.) *Culture and Management*, Harmondsworth, Middx: Penguin.

Weiss, Richard M. and Mille, Lynn E. (1987) 'The Concept of Ideology in Organizational Analysis', *Academy of Management Review* 12: 104–16.

Weitzel, W. and Jonsson, E. (1989) 'Decline in Organizations: A Literature Integration and Extension', *Administrative Science Quarterly* 34: 91–109.

Westin, Alan F. (1983) 'The United States Bill of Rights and the Canadian Charter: A Socio-Political Analysis', in William R. McKercher (ed.) *The U.S. Bill of Rights and the Canadian Charter of Rights and Freedoms*, Toronto: Ontario Economic Council.

Weston, Rae (1980) *Domestic and Multinational Banking: The Effects of Monetary Policy*, New York:Columbia University Press.

Whetten, David A (1980) 'Organizational Decline: A Neglected Topic in Organizational Science', *Academy of Management Review* 5(4): 577–88.

Wildavsky, Aaron (1972) 'The Self-Evaluating Organization', *Public Administration Review* 32: 509–20.

Wilensky, Harold (1969) *Organizational Intelligence*, New York: Basic Books.

Williams, M.J. (1988) 'The Comeback of Bob Abboud', *Fortune* 29 February: 91–5.

Williamson, Oliver E. (1963) 'Models of Rational Managerial Behavior', in Richard Cyert and James March (eds) *The Behavioral Theory of the Firm*, Englewood Cliffs, N.J.: Prentice-Hall.

—— (1970) *Corporate Control and Business Behavior*, Englewood Cliffs, N.J.: Prentice-Hall.

Wittinck, Dick R. (1988) *The Application of Regression Analysis*, Needham Heights, Mass.: Allyn and Bacon, Inc.

Woerheide, Walt (1980) *Economies of Scale in the SLA Industry: The Historical Record*, Federal Home Loan Bank Board, Office of Policy and Economic Research Working Paper 92. Washington, D.C.: FHLBB.

Woodward, Joan (1969) 'Management and Technology', in Tom Burns (ed.) *Industrial Man*, Baltimore, Md.: Penguin Books.

Zald, Mayer N. (ed.) (1970) *Power in Organizations*, Nashville, Tenn.: Vanderbilt University Press.

Zey, Mary (ed.) (1992) *Decision Making: Alternatives to Rational Choice Models* Newbury Park, Calif.: Sage.

Ziegel, Jacob S., Waverman, Leonard and Conklin, David W. (eds) (1985) *Canadian Financial Institutions: Changing the Regulatory Environment*, Toronto: Ontario Economic Council.

Zimmerman, Frederick M. (1991) *The Turnaround Experience*, New York: McGraw-Hill.

Zysman, John (1983) *Financial Systems and the Politics of Industrial Change*, Ithaca, N.Y.: Cornell University Press.

DATA SOURCES

Bank of Montreal, *Annual Report*, Montreal: 1973–83.

Bank of Nova Scotia, *Annual Report*, Halifax: 1973–83.

Bankers Trust Company, *Annual Report*, New York: 1973–83.

Bramalea Development Company, *Annual Report*, Toronto: 1973–83.

Cadillac-Fairview Corporation, *Annual Report*, Toronto: 1975–83.

Campeau Corp. Ltd, *Annual Report*, Ottawa: 1973–83.

Canada. Department of Finance *Report of the Superintendent of Insurance for Canada: Trust and Loan Companies*, Ottawa: Dept of Supply and Service: 1972 through 1982.

Canada Permanent Trustco *Annual Report*, Toronto: 1973–83.

Canada Trustco *Annual Report*, London, Ont.: 1973–83.

Canadian Imperial Bank of Commerce, *Annual Report*, Toronto: 1973–83.

Continental Illinois Corporation, *Annual Report*, Chicago: 1973–83.

Cousins Properties Incorporated (Atlanta), '10K Report', Washington: Disclosure (microfiche), 1972–82.

Daon Development Corp., *Annual Report*, Vancouver: 1973–83.

Development Corporation of America (Hollywood, Fla.). '10K Report', Washington: Disclosure (microfiche), 1972–82.

Financial Post, *Survey of Industrials*, Toronto: Financial Post, 1972–82.

First Chicago Corporation, *Annual Report*, Chicago: 1973–83.

Manufacturers Hanover Corporation, *Annual Report*, New York: 1973–83.

Marine Midland Banks Inc., *Annual Report*, Buffalo: 1973–83.

Montreal Trustco, *Annual Report*, Montreal: 1973–83.

Moody's Bank and Finance Manual, New York: Moody's Investor's Service, 1972–83.

Moody's Industrial Manual, New York: Moody's Investor's Service, 1972–83.

Mortgage Insurance Company of Canada, *Annual Report*, Toronto: 1973–83.

National Trustco, *Annual Report*, Toronto: 1973–83.

Nuwest Group Ltd, *Annual Report*, Calgary: 1973–83.

Royal Bank of Canada, *Annual Report*, Montreal: 1973–83.

Royal Trustco, *Annual Report*, Ottawa: 1973–83.

Ryan Homes Inc. (Pittsburgh), '10K Report', Washington: Disclosure (micro-fiche), 1972–82.

Standard and Poor's Register of Corporations, Directors and Executives (3 Vols) New York: Standard and Poor's Corporation, 1972–83.

Starrett Housing Corporation (New York), '10K Report', Washington: Disclosure (microfiche), 1972–82.

Toronto-Dominion Bank, *Annual Report*, Toronto: 1973–83.

TRIZEC Construction Ltd, *Annual Report*, Calgary: 1973–83.

U.S. Home Corporation (Houston, Texas), '10K Report', Washington: Disclosure (microfiche), 1972–82.

Victoria and Grey Trust Co., *Annual Report*, Stratford, Ont.: 1973–83.

Index